Storm and Sorrow in the High Pamirs

ROBERT W. CRAIG

Storm and Sorrow in the High Pamirs

SIMON AND SCHUSTER

NEW YORK

Published by Simon and Schuster
A Division of Gulf & Western Corporation
Simon & Schuster Building
Rockefeller Center
1230 Avenue of the Americas
New York, New York 10020
SIMON AND SCHUSTER and colophon are trademarks of Simon & Schuster

Designed by Elizabeth Woll
Manufactured in the United States of America

1   2   3   4   5   6   7   8   9   10

Library of Congress Cataloging in Publication Data

Craig, Robert W
    Storm and sorrow in the high Pamirs.

    1. Mountaineering—Pamir.   2. Pamir—Description.
3.   Craig, Robert W.   4. Mountaineers—United
States—Biography.   5. Mountaineering—Russia.
I. Title.
GV199.44.P3C7   1980   796.5′22′09586   80-13289
ISBN 0-671-25154-6

This book is dedicated
to the memory of Gary Ullin,
Eva Eissenschmidt, the eight Soviet
women, and the five Estonians.

▲

Additionally, I would like to
dedicate it to my three children,
Kathleen, Jennifer, and Michael.

▲

and, because it was one
of his last great adventures,
I hope it will commemorate the
memory of Bruce Carson, who,
in his last few years, brought
so much to American mountaineering.

▲
Contents

▲
Preface

When *Storm and Sorrow* was first published in 1978, there was little expectation that it would have much of an audience beyond the limited literary fraternity of climbers and "armchair mountaineers." However, judging by a surprising number of enthusiastic letters and the sellout of the Mountaineer Publishing Company's edition, the book seems to have struck an unexpected chord among the public at large. We are grateful for this and can only hope it will continue to shed faint light on why men and women climb mountains.

The 1974 American Pamirs/U.S.S.R. Expedition is long past and not particularly distinguished in mountaineering history. But what happened in the course of that summer does deserve recording, for there was much courage in the face of an unusual chain of events somehow beyond the control of the participants, and a kind of beauty that emerged from the ruin of all their hopes.

I have been helped greatly in tracing the sequence of events by virtually all the members of the American expedition. Jock Glidden, John Evans, Allen Steck, Jeff Lowe, Bruce Carson, Molly Higgins, Peter Lev, and John Roskelley maintained diaries and shared these with me. The quality of these entries adds, in my estimation, immeasurably to the book. They also reviewed the manuscript in draft, as did Peter Schoening and Jed Williamson. I am grateful for their many valuable suggestions.

Grant Barnes, Chairman of Publications of the American Alpine Club, was of untiring assistance in preparing the manuscript and in arranging publication.

Dee Molenaar, my friend and tentmate of K2 days, did maps and illustrations that bring this book as close to reality for the reader as any of the photographs do.

Other friends who have offered counsel and guidance and above all candor in making this book an honest chronicle have been too numerous to mention in these pages, but they will each know my gratitude. I am, however, especially indebted to my closest friend, John J. Carmody of the Washington *Post*, for his toughness in helping me strike what I hope were the proper balances in tone and direction.

Sidney Urquhart suggested I seek simplicity over cleverness and the portrayal of people over rhetoric. I can only hope I have partially succeeded.

Jean Paul Zuanon's book *Pamir* was very helpful in confirming events and chronology. I was grateful for the patience and understanding of my friend and associate Robert Maynard of Keystone.

I would also like to thank Penny Banks and June Lindenmayer for their help in the preparation of the first edition. Additionally, I would like to thank Deborah Womeldorf for her assistance in the manuscript for this new edition.

The Literary Fund Committee of The Mountaineers in Seattle was helpful in many ways in the preparation and

execution of the original edition. Connie Pious, James San-
ford and John Pollack were especially supportive.

Now the book is being brought out in a new edition by
Simon and Schuster, and I have been helped tremendously in making it a simpler, more understandable story
by Susan Bolotin, Editor in Chief of Touchstone Books.

▲
Introduction

There is very little in the world that isn't climbed. Walls and summits are approached in places as remote and as unlikely as the Amazon Basin, New Guinea, Greenland, Equatorial Africa, Central Antarctica, the Soviet-Chinese border, Baffin Land, snake-infested rock outcroppings of Australia, and the surrealistic spires of Patagonia. They are all hard climbs, some are even called "desperate," but most are not invested with the drama and mystery of George Mallory approaching the Second Step of Everest. George Mallory and Andrew Irvine were last seen by Noel Odell moving slowly at about 28,250 feet at 2:30 P.M., May 31, 1924, as they were about to try the technically difficult Second Step, a 300-foot rock buttress on the north ridge of Mount Everest, and the last real obstacle to the highest summit in the world. Swirling clouds, blowing snow enveloped them as Odell looked on, and they were never seen again. Years later an ice axe believed to be Mallory's was found at about 27,000 feet. Did they reach the summit? Where and when did they fall? That was the

15

ultimate unknown. The age of discovery and conquest has given way to a new period of personal and creative mountaineering.

There are still a great many walls of rock and ice and a diminishing number of high summits that haven't been touched, but these are going rapidly to talented young climbers from every part of the world seeking the untried or that which has not been done. What is creative about these routes and ascents is the style in which they are done.

Routes that previously were climbed by means of technical aids such as expansion bolts and stirrup slings for ascending are now done "free," or without artificial assistance, by the extension of climbing techniques to what might be thought of as the outer limit of physical capability. Large, very high peaks that were formerly climbed only by large-scale expeditions and siege tactics are now being approached by small, compact teams carrying virtually everything on their backs in what we know as "alpine-style" assaults. In what might be called the "classical period" of mountaineering, the highest peaks were invariably attacked from what was believed to be their easiest sides. Now alpine-style strategies permit climbing teams to try even the hardest faces and ridges of the great mountains. Alpine style really means going as light as possible, even on Himalayan peaks, carrying each camp in effect up to the next, and never leaving any fixed camp in place save the highest.

Over the years, a great deal of the most satisfying mountaineering has been done on a smaller scale than that of the major expeditions. Teams of two to six climbers, usually friends, traveling light, using few or no porters, perhaps using airdrops, are far more mobile and in some respects more effective than the militarylike operations that have characterized Everest, K2, Kanchenjunga, Makalu, and Dhaulagiri.

In July 1974, four teams, each derived from a total American expedition of nineteen climbers to the Soviet Union, found themselves in position in the central Pamirs Range to do alpine-style unclimbed routes on the high ice mountains athwart the Soviet-Chinese frontier. No American and few Europeans had ever climbed in those mountains before.

This is a region rich in legends of spirit people and demons who reside in, and dominate, the foreboding heights. Within the legends is the belief that the rivers and lakes of the region are inhabited by godlike beings who, if not actually gods, have supernatural powers. For the people who live here, the belief has persisted until very recently, if not to the present, that the rivers are ruled by the Almasde Demon, the lord of the whirlpool. The lakes, it is said, are inhabited by hairy mermaids and mermen, immensely rich in gold and precious stones.

Operating from an extremely well organized base camp that was set up by the Russians in a flower-carpeted, treeless alpine meadow at 11,700 feet, 160 climbers from twelve nations were distributed broadly over the high, ice-covered, and unexpectedly stormbound Bam-i-dunya, or the "Roof of the World," as this legendary range was known by the ancient Vakhans and by those worshipers of the Parsee faith from Persia who settled there several millennia earlier.

The American Alpine Club, through its board of directors, had asked Peter Schoening to lead a team of American climbers to the Soviet Union in the summer of 1974. He was to be assisted in the organization of this effort by Allen Steck, Samuel Silverstein, M.D., and myself. Later, as the tasks of expeditionary organization grew and became more defined, I was to assume the job of deputy leader.

There had been much on-again, off-again negotiation from 1972 forward, and finally in 1974 we found ourselves, nineteen Americans strong, in Moscow coming face to face not only with the members of the Soviet Federation of Mountaineering, but with climbing teams from Scotland, France, the Netherlands, Italy, Switzerland, England, Germany, and Japan.

Each group had arrived expecting to enjoy a degree of solitariness and isolation after the formalities of the official Soviet Base Camp, plunging into diverse parts of the vast and not entirely explored Pamirs. To a degree this was to prove true, but, in spite of separate agreements made earlier with the Soviets, the pervading atmosphere of the International Camp, at least as seen by the Soviets, was that of a world gathering of climbers come to the Pamirs to share in the celebration of climbing a great symbol of their culture and sport, Peak Lenin. In all fairness, the Soviets held scrupulously to the agreements previously made, but one sensed they were not really comfortable with the goals of the egocentric, individualistic Westerners.

The sheer number and variety of nationalities delighted the Soviets, and they would tout the gathering as the greatest assemblage of climbers in history. But the capability and quality of the mountaineers were by no means even. Some of the very best and a good many who didn't begin to qualify as first-rate climbers—through no fault of their own—were there. Whatever their backgrounds and abilities, they all nourished great hopes and ambitions for the summer. How quickly these bright hopes and visions of triumph would turn to bitter disappointment, despair, tragedy and grief!

This is a chronicle not of an expedition, not of a single climb, but of a complex of events that included many climbs, much suffering and death, and struggles for life against odds that were greater than any of the participants could know. This is the story of midsummer tragedy in the Pamirs.

CHAPTER ONE

▲

History, Frustration, and Fulfillment

Since the 1930s, American mountaineers had sought opportunities to climb on Russian mountains, to climb with Russian climbers, and to exchange literature of mutual interest. In 1974, there were only three books in the English language about mountaineering in Russia available in the mountaineering libraries of the United States. They were *Red Peak* by Malcolm Slesser, *Red Snows* by Lord Hunt, and *The Ascent of Mount Stalin* by Michael Romm. There were no photographic archives. These British books had painted a rather forbidding picture of climbing in the Soviet Union, and one wondered whether the legendary peaks of the U.S.S.R. might be worth the effort.

For a good many years, American requests for permission to climb in the Caucasus of the southwestern Soviet Union, the Pamirs, and the Tien Shan Range along the frontier with China had met with polite disinterest. The Soviets had good cause to be particularly sensitive about their Asiatic interior; the Caucasus and Pamirs must have seemed vital security areas in the '50s and '60s. Crises along the vast Soviet-Chinese border only seemed to intensify the sensitivity.

A thaw toward the West, in mountaineering at least, developed in 1962, when the Soviets invited an English-Scottish expedition to join forces with a group of Soviet climbers in an attempt on a new route on Peak of Communism (Pik Kommunizma), 24,590 feet, formerly known as Mount Stalin. As a consequence, a strong group of British (Scottish and English) climbers went to the Pamirs in 1962 and did climb Communism and several other peaks in the north-central Pamirs. But the joint expedition, led on the British side by Lord Hunt, and on the Scottish, by Professor Malcolm Slesser, was marred by the deaths of two of the finest British climbers of that era, Robin Smith and Wilfrid Noyce. In subsequent years of the 1960s, a British team was allowed to climb in the Caucasus and two Austrian groups visited the Pamirs.

In the late '60s, Soviet and American mountaineering representatives had met in Europe at meetings of the Union Internationale des Associations d'Alpinisme (UIAA). Fritz Weissner, one of the most famous and universally respected climbers in mountaineering history, represented the American Alpine Club (AAC) in early discussion with such Soviet delegates as Vitaly Abalakov, V. Borovikov and Eugene Gippenreiter. John L. J. Hart, then President of the American Alpine Club, attended a meeting of the UIAA in Tbilisi in the Soviet Union. Jerry Hart, as a matter of fact, was an essential link to the future success of all American-Soviet exchanges owing to his admirable patience and doggedness in keeping the channels of communication and cooperation open. As a consequence of these several efforts, the groundwork was laid for the American visit to the Soviet Union in 1974.

The board of the AAC, on receiving a cable from Borovikov inviting the Americans to visit the Pamirs, voted to undertake the organization of a team of the best American climbers who could be assembled. Peter Schoening as leader and I as deputy were to have the primary responsibilities and be assisted in the organizational efforts by Samuel Silverstein and Allen Steck.

At the time of the Soviet Federation–American Alpine Club negotiations and for some time before, there had been mounting criticism that the AAC had done little to stimulate and encourage expeditionary climbing among the American climbing community as a whole and the younger climbers of the country in particular. Chris Jones characterized this feeling in his tough article in *Ascent* magazine, "Who Needs the AAC." Jones commented:

> The greatest single expense for parties climbing in distant ranges is often the air fare. With the increase in charter and group travel, the club could offer reduced-cost flights not only to the Alps and the Andes, but also the Himalayas. In this way small groups, who have no desire to go in for publicity and fund-raising campaigns, might well be enabled to climb in the ultimate mountains—the Himalayas.
>
> Finally a progressive club would be able to begin a mountaineering fund similar to the Mount Everest Foundation in Britain. The MEF arose from the financially successful 1953 Everest climb, and now uses that money in turn to support numerous parties, both large and small, on worthwhile enterprises. Certain groups, such as the recent Annapurna South Face Expedition, have considerable support from the MEF, and will thus return a portion of their profits to the MEF to be used once again.

Because of the anticipated numbers the Soviets would accept and the low cost per climber that had been indicated by the Soviets, it was hoped that a quite large, representative American group could be put in the field.

The American Pamirs expedition from the outset was seen as the beginning of a Soviet Union–United States exchange that had great potential for the stimulation and development of younger mountaineers, not to mention for establishing ongoing relations in the sport of mountaineering between the two countries. These younger American mountaineers—who would form the majority of the American expedition—would also become the leaders of American mountaineering for the foreseeable future. In the company of a few veterans, they could gain new experience in planning and executing small-scale expeditions in very high mountains without the backbreaking problems of access to restricted foreign ranges, funding, and official endorsement. Those problems would be the primary responsibility of the organizing team of Schoening, Craig, Silverstein, and Steck.

Indeed, out of the 1973–74 efforts which culminated in the American Pamirs/U.S.S.R. Expedition have come three subsequent Soviet Mountaineering Federation–American Alpine Club exchanges. In the first, in 1975, six top Soviet alpinists visited the United States, climbing hard routes in a wide range of areas, from the cliffs of the Shawangunks in New York and the Tetons in Wyoming to the North Cascades of Washington and the incomparable walls of Yosemite. The second reciprocal exchange in 1976 found six of the best U.S. climbers back in the U.S.S.R. doing a wide variety of hard-rock and ice climbs, from the Pamirs-Alai to the Tien Shan and the Caucasus. The Soviets returned to the U.S. in 1977 and achieved their objectives of major climbs in Alaska and Washington State. In 1978, a team of six Americans paid a return visit to the Pamirs and climbed Peak of Communism by a hard route.

The original indications by the Soviets suggested that a fairly large roster of American climbers for the Pamirs would be agreeable to them, but by 1973, when Borovikov's cable arrived, the number inexplicably had dwindled to twelve. Pete and I felt very strongly that a larger complement was essential if we were to achieve the goal of making the Pamirs expedition a training experience for talented young American climbers. We felt, as well, that female American climbers should be a part of the roster and that an ideal number for the team would be somewhere between eighteen and twenty-four.

With twelve places to fill, four of whom were identified at the outset, we began to solicit applications via the *Climbing News* of the AAC, and through notices to the various sections of the club and other climbing organizations. We specified the applications should include names of other endorsing climbers as well as records of significant climbs and mountaineering experience. We made it very clear that membership in the American Alpine Club was in no way a requisite to selection for the team.

Within about five weeks of broadcasting news of the Pamirs expedition we were inundated with applications from an outstanding cross section of American climbers. To this list Pete, Sam, Al, and I added a few more carefully sought out names of climbers we had reason to believe might be reluctant or unwilling to apply, but who would add immense strength if chosen on the basis of all the criteria. Three of these actually joined the group by the end of the selection process.

It was obvious that we needed more places on the team, but communications with Moscow were so fragmentary and unclear—letters and telegrams often were unanswered or, if answered, not understood—that it was decided Pete should go to Moscow to nail down once and for all the terms of our visit, the number of Americans who would be acceptable to the Soviets, and the climbing objectives we would be permitted to attempt.

By this time, autumn of 1973 had passed and we were in the beginning weeks of 1974. A good deal had been accomplished: we had developed an excellent potential roster of climbers out of more than 200 well-qualified applicants; we had in hand or in pledges more than $40,000 of the estimated $60,000 we would need; and we had begun

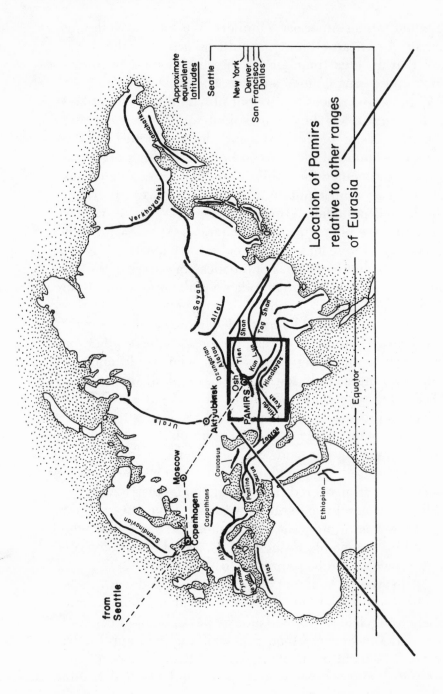

Location of Pamirs
relative to other ranges
of Eurasia

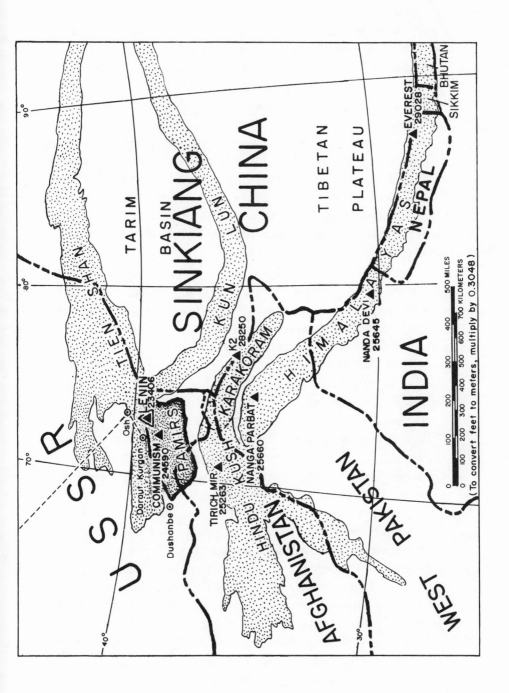

equipment procurement that assured us of being ready for departure to the Soviet Union in July as an expedition composed of several self-contained alpine-style teams.

Pete flew to a damp and cold Moscow in early April. He had little advance information as to what to expect, save that the Soviet Federation of Mountaineering officials were not mere bureaucrats, but mountaineers first and foremost. He met with Vitaly Abalakov, the father of Soviet mountaineering; Michael Monastyrski, director of the Soviet Federation's mountaineering camps in the Pamirs and Caucasus; and Dr. Eugene Gippenreiter, Secretary for International Affairs of the Soviet Federation of Mountaineering.

In very short order Pete's hosts in Moscow provided answers to our basic questions. We could bring a team of nineteen American climbers. We were also given assurances that four requested unclimbed and untried climbing objectives would be exclusively designated for first attempts by the American teams. Pete was told that the Federation members felt we might be able to bring our crucial radios to Moscow despite the usual government restrictions against foreign electronic devices.

Pete got a more specific sense of the summer that lay ahead for us. The Soviets had planned an international gathering of mountaineering teams from a number of Western European countries and Japan as well as several from Eastern Europe and republics of the Soviet Union. The Soviets were particularly emphatic that the presence of the various climbing groups, presumably to operate as independent teams much as our own, would not in any way inhibit the American "pioneer ascents," as they call unclimbed routes. Pete wondered precisely what the other teams might be doing, but felt it might be impolite to ask.

The Federation officials showed Pete various points of interest in Moscow and hosted him at a small cheerful dinner. Curiously, though he tried very hard to obtain reasonably good photographs of the Pamirs, there were virtually none to be had, and he returned with three or four black and white contact prints that would not have qualified in a photographic contest in the 1860s. Virtually no detail of routes appeared. Yet we had seen photos of the highest fidelity of Soviet astronauts in space. After we arrived in Moscow, we discovered that the Soviet Federation had produced an elaborate four-color brochure announcing the "International Alpiniade" in the Pamirs. The piece was printed in English, French, and German and had excellent photographs of several of the routes we hoped to attempt. Was there some message to this? We wondered if this was the closed society in action, the ultimate distrust of the Soviet Union for the United States. Could the Soviets have feared we might not appear if there was any possibility the venture might evolve into a competitive situation between different national teams vying for the best routes? Was there the equally unappealing possibility of the Soviets' requiring everyone to climb Peak Lenin by one of its easy standard routes? We never really found out.

Once Pete was back in the States, he and I spent many hours on the telephone engaged in the final selection process. Our criteria for selection had been simple: outstanding mountaineering skills (but sheer virtuosity would not necessarily outweigh other factors); geographical diversity within the group (we sought and obtained representation of all major U.S. climbing areas); and the less tangible but essential personal qualities of compatibility, cheerfulness, and humor that would likely result in a happy group. More expeditions, large and small, have foundered from dissension than perhaps from any other cause. Now we had to add seven more climbers to our original roster of twelve.

There is no way to ensure compatibility. In the last analysis, it comes down to the gut feelings of the expedition leader about an individual man or woman. There are many technical climbers who, in the context of intense involvement on a big wall, or solving a singular alpine route of the highest standard, are superior but simply do not make the grade on an expedition. For a variety of psychological reasons, they are likely to be miserable and ultimately make everyone around them miserable. In high mountains, the consequences of rationalizing high technical ability against unselfishness, which is what compatibility really comes down to, are very harsh. Perhaps compassion is a better word than unselfishness. Toughness is an element too; it can co-exist with unselfishness and must always be simultaneously sought in making up an expedition roster. In even the best teams only about half of the members will really combine toughness and compassion.

The expedition roster that emerged had strong people, diverse in nature and cheerful. The various members did not climb continuously together as a single team; rather, several combinations were tried before we reached the Soviet Union. As it turned out, the selection principles that had guided us still held up, and the Americans who went to the Pamirs aquitted themselves very well during a very strange summer.

Bruce Carson, at 21, was a sometime physics and liberal arts student who climbed mountains as if they were in themselves art forms. In a very few seasons, he had become one of the country's most creative solo climbers and one who, with Yvon Chouinard, pioneered a completely clean ascent of the "Nose" of El Capitan in Yosemite Valley. He was one of the new breed, both talented athletically and a special spirit as well. He died a year after the Pamirs expedition when a cornice collapsed with him on a summit of Trisul in the Garwhal-Himalayas.

John Evans, 35, the program director of the Colorado Outward Bound School, is the rare combination of a pioneer big-wall climber and a heavily seasoned expedition climber who had been to the Yukon, Antarctica, and had failed on the southwest face of Everest. He was in many

28

ways the strongest individual climber some of us had ever seen. He left in Denver a wife and newborn daughter.

Jocelyn (Jock) Glidden had done notable big-wall climbs in North America, Peru, and Alaska. A professor of philosophy, married, and the father of two children, Jock at 38 was the eccentric, quietly blithe spirit of the expedition. He had an uncorrupted belief that mountains were climbed solely for themselves.

Molly Higgins, 25, was really the "baby" of the U.S. team and, though mature enough to have been an instructor in Outward Bound, had probably the least overall mountaineering background of the expedition at the late moment when she was swept into the Pamirs experience. She acquitted herself exceptionally well in the U.S.S.R. and has since become one of the premiere women climbers in the country.

Marty Hoey was at 24 a Mount Rainier guide and a graduate student in education at the University of Washington. Marty was thoroughly experienced in alpine climbing and was a strong member of the American team. She has continued high climbing and was a member of the 1976 Nanda Devi Himalayan Expedition in India.

Chris Kopczynski, 28, was a building contractor from Spokane, a strong, seasoned alpine climber who had had distinguished climbs in the Cascades and Canada. Chris was married and the father of a seven-year-old daughter. On the way home from the U.S.S.R., he and another Pamir teammate, John Roskelley, did the feared north face of the Eiger in Switzerland. Chris, in many ways the shyest member of the expedition, was also one of the most willing to help his various teammates.

Peter Lev, 34, lived the ideal life, being an avalanche ranger at Alta in the winter and mountain guide in the Tetons in the summer. Another big-wall climber, though more of a total mountaineer, Lev's record included climbs in Yosemite, Alaska, Canada, and Dhaulagiri and Nanda

Devi in the Himalayas. Pete was one of the most serious and inner-directed of the climbers.

Jeff Lowe, 22, a sometime student, former ski racer, mountain guide, and probably the best of a new breed of ice climbers in the U.S., had considerable big-wall experience as well as several major Canadian north face ascents to his credit. The whimsical Lowe was always the source of a laugh or friendly smile.

John Marts, 26, was a very broadly experienced rock and ice climber who had done the Walker spur of the Grandes Jorasses in the French Alps at nineteen and had pioneered many major routes in the Northwest. Marts, wryly humorous and quick-witted, worked for several months to ensure that the expedition and personal equipment met the best standards. Since his journey to the U.S.S.R., Marts has gone on to finish law school at Gonzaga University.

John Roskelley, 26, is probably the most prodigious climber in America. Brilliant on both ice and rock, he was one of two Americans to reach the summit of Dhaulagiri (26,810 feet) in 1973. John had done a wide variety of major big-wall climbs. In 1976, he led the very difficult north face of Nanda Devi. In 1978, he reached the summit of K2 (28,250 feet), the second-highest mountain in the world. Married, Roskelley is as complex as he is strong.

Frank Sarnquist came to the expedition late, as Sam Silverstein had to withdraw as our physician. Few teams have been so fortunate in finding a gifted replacement for a team member. Frank, 33 and married, was an anesthesiologist, a former guide, and an all-around mountaineer with broad experience in Yosemite, Alaska, Peru and the Himalayas. Slightly taciturn, compact, and strong as an ox, Frank was invariably cheerful.

Fred Stanley, 32, married, father of two small children and a mountain guide turned computer programmer, was an excellent all-around mountaineer with a fine record of ascents in the western U.S., and with several outstanding ice routes on Rainier. He was a member of the luckless 1975 K2 expedition. One of the keen wits of the expedition, Fred was a cool hand in times of trouble.

Peter Schoening, 48, the expedition leader, a chemical engineer, was one of the best mountaineers who developed in the post–World War II period. He had distinguished himself on K2, and was one of the first two Americans to climb an 8,000-meter peak (first ascent of Gasherbrum I in the Karakoram-Himalayas of Pakistan), as well as having done many other major routes in Alaska, Canada, and the U.S. Pete had also served as co-leader of a very successful Antarctic expedition. Enormously strong, a good technician, and a great spirit, Peter put endless hours of effort into the expedition.

Al Steck, 47, founder of Mountain Travel, Inc., was another of the historic climbers, having pioneered big walls in Yosemite and participated in expeditions in the Himalayas, Alaska, Peru, and the Hindu Kush. Soft-spoken, impish at times, Al was always one of the strengths of the Pamirs expedition. Married and the father of two college students, Steck led the 1976 Pakistani ascent of the dazzling Paiju in the Karakoram.

Gary Ullin, 31, a former Rainier guide, was an airline pilot. Gary was one of the strongest members of the expedition, a mountaineer of great versatility, having helped lead a brilliant first ascent of the east ridge of Mount St. Elias in Alaska. He had climbed as well in South America and on Mount Kenya in Africa. Unfailingly cheerful and generous, often very funny, Gary had a very serious, poetic side.

Jed Williamson, 33, a New Hampshire schoolteacher and educational consultant, had guided on Rainier and done extensive expeditionary climbing in Alaska, including a new route on McKinley and explorations in the Brooks Range. Witty and a storyteller of real ability, Jed was as well a very sensitive teammate. In stressful times he made his companions laugh when it was badly needed. Jed is married and the father of two small children. He is chairman of the prestigious Safety Committee of the American Alpine Club.

Christopher Wren, 36, *New York Times* Moscow correspondent, married and the father of two, had climbed in Alaska (McKinley) as well as the western U.S. and Europe. Though not the most experienced climber on the expedition, Chris acquitted himself well on Peak Lenin and was invaluable in handling logistical matters on the ground in Moscow as well as in interpreting Russian-English conversation. Chris was one of the more sophisticated yet quiet members.

Michael Yokell, 31, an economist, is a strong, versatile big-wall climber who has done the Salathe in Yosemite, the Diamond (Longs Peak), climbs in Alaska and Peru, and large-scale alpine climbs in the Alps. Michael, very intense, one of our two Russian linguists, had done a great deal of very hard climbing with his talented alpinist wife, Jane Bunin. He joined the expedition in Copenhagen on our way to the U.S.S.R.

My own background included the fact that I was, at 50, the oldest member of the expedition. I had climbed extensively in Alaska, Canada, and the U.S., and had been a member of the 1953 American K2 expedition. I had been a guide on Rainier, done one of the earliest ascents of Shiprock and Mount McKinley, and the first ascent of Devil's Thumb in the Coast Range of Alaska.

The climbers we had chosen were as individually distinct yet homogeneous as any large team of mountaineers who ever set off for high places. We were quite sure the essential quality of compatibility we sought was there in every climber, but we could only really know what we had when we got into the mountains. We hoped to get an advance sense of our people and possible team combinations, not to mention seven days of essential acclimatization, when we took the expedition to the top of Rainier the first week in July.

The major projects began at the inception of the expedition and continued until our departure: equipment design, development, and procurement and the essential fund-raising effort. We had a good deal of talent in the equipment area and set John Marts and Bruce Carson to the tasks of personal kits as well as alpine-style team gear. It was their responsibility to seek out insights and suggestions from other team members. We encouraged them to allow for a certain degree of individual choice in boots, climbing pants, and overboots. The range of personal preference in foot gear is especially wide, and the number of different kinds of climbing boots almost equalled the number of team members. Sam Silverstein established criteria for individual and team medical kits. We left the matter of food to be settled until we got a clearer determination of the nature of the food we had been vaguely informed the Soviets would provide. Pete had learned in Moscow that the Soviet Federation would provide total food supplies for the various teams, but a few of us were apprehensive that too much would be at stake if the diet was not compatible with American tastes.

Fund raising is crucial for any expedition. Usually, for a large undertaking—which the American Pamirs expedition certainly was—groups begin to secure underwriting a year and a half to two years in advance of the climb. We had eight months. Pete and I had the primary responsibility of finding the money. We could encourage the team members to turn up whatever they could, but the reality, given the time frame, was that we needed substantial contributions and we needed them fast. For the size of the expedition, the objectives, and the distance to be traveled, the actual amount needed was remarkably modest. We estimated we could cover everything for about $60,000.

The American Alpine Club was in tough financial straits

with the decline in market value of its endowment port-
folio, not to mention earnings of its shares, and clearly
could not help the expedition other than to provide spon-
sorship and moral support. Pete conceived of a brilliant
approach that he managed to sell to Eddie Bauer Outfitters
and that provided at the outset $25,000 in funding. This
pledge was given fairly early and literally made the initial
equipment acquisitions possible.

Under this exceptionally creative gift, Eddie Bauer out-
fitted the expedition, providing all items of equipment
specified by the expedition, such as tentage, sleeping bags,
down jackets, wind suits, cagoules, boots, super-gaitors,
and climbing hardware. These items were purchased on
the "best available design" basis, and were obtained at
cost. The arrangement proved very flexible and the equipment performed extremely well; the contribution was not
only generous, but enlightened.

We approached various publications and publishers in
hopes of advances on articles or books, but time again
proved too short. Further, if one is really honest about it,
the nebulous nature of our enterprise in the Pamirs must
have left most publishers somewhat unenthralled. We
turned to the U.S. Department of State for cultural exchange funds, but couldn't seem to turn up anyone at State
who had any inkling of what mountaineering was about or
who knew that in the Soviet Union mountaineering claims
five million devotees at various levels of proficiency.

We then approached a number of U.S. corporations involved in trade or pursuing trade relations with the
U.S.S.R., thinking that support of an expedition fostering
U.S.-Soviet understanding could not but help improve
their image in the U.S.S.R. This process led us on many
fruitless searches until we found one corporation and its
president who believed in the value of our project and its
potential for the company's image.

Johns-Manville Corporation was actively negotiating extensive trade contracts in Eastern Europe and the Soviet Union when we approached Dr. Richard Goodwin, who was then president of the company. A lover of the mountains, Goodwin was as well a hard bargainer for Johns-Manville, and we can only hope the Soviets recognized the farsighted gift of $15,000 as something that assured a breakthrough in U.S.-U.S.S.R. relations. With that gift, which arrived little more than two months before our departure, we knew we could raise the total amount needed. We were on our way.

Work on equipment, procurement of high-frequency two-way radios, insuring equipment, final preparation of medical kits, and gathering supplemental food to be used with the Russian diet continued through the winter and spring, virtually until departure time. Each climber had personal items of responsibility, but was especially charged with being in top physical condition by the time of arrival in Seattle.

On July 2, we gathered in Seattle at the home of Peter and Maryanne Schoening for a farewell dinner and a get-acquainted meeting; that meeting would continue in earnest the next several days as we climbed to the summit of Mount Rainier (14,410 feet) for a period of acclimatization just prior to our departure for Moscow. Everything was behind us now—training, personal outfitting, the assembling of equipment, airline tickets, passports, and visas; everyone and everything seemed in good order. Two members of the expedition would meet us in Europe—Mike Yokell in Copenhagen and Chris Wren in Moscow.

The group was in good spirits, and much joshing—particularly about one's poor physical condition—and laughter percolated among the members even as several met for the first time. Some had been together in smaller aggregations before: Lev and Roskelley, Williamson and Lev, Williamson and Ullin, Roskelley and Marts, Glidden and Lowe, Evans and Lowe, Lev and Glidden, Schoening and

Evans, Schoening and Stanley, Ullin and Stanley, Kop-czynski and Roskelley, Steck and Evans, and Sarnquist and Steck. I had climbed with Lev, Schoening, Stanley, Steck, and Yokell. Considerable cohesiveness seemed to have been brought into the expedition through these chance shared experiences over the years. Although it hadn't con-sciously entered into our planning, it undoubtedly contrib-uted to the speed and smoothness with which the overall group came together as an expedition and as members of the climbing teams.

The true beginning of the expedition was on Mount Rainier. Other expeditions have utilized Rainier as a train-ing and testing ground, notably the 1963 American Mount Everest team, and more recently, the 1975 K2 expedition, but these occasions were separated in each case by about a year from the main expeditionary effort. The American Pamirs expedition commenced on Rainier with only a three-and-a-half-day pause between the 14,410-foot sum-mit of that mountain and the 11,700-foot Base Camp in the Achik Tash Valley.

The terms of the Soviet invitation to climb in the Pamirs were quite fair, but very much limited by time. Once in the U.S.S.R., all transportation costs, lodging enroute to and from the Pamirs, and food would be covered by a charge of $750 per climber. Transportation to and from the U.S.S.R. was additional, but all in all, our cost per man including equipment was under $2,500. The really harsh consideration was that we would have at best 32 days in which to achieve our goals of making four of the hardest climbs and explorations in the Soviet Union.

Normally, 32 days are not insufficient time for a series of alpine-style high-altitude climbs, but it could be close where teams would be doing climbs in excess of 20,000 feet on terrain they had never seen, and for which they had no reconnaissance photographs or significant descriptive data. Acclimatization itself could take two or even three weeks, and then any meaningful margin of climbing time would be gone.

Mount Rainier added a week—probably the effects of two in terms of acclimatization—to our physiological and psychological adaptation, and provided a shakedown of equipment, a demonstration of personalities and workable combinations under stress, and an expeditionary momentum that would be invaluable once the Soviet Base Camp was reached. Future expeditions would do well to consider such strategy where time is short and acclimatization is crucial. It should be noted, however, that a day of living or travel at sea level more or less negates a day of high-altitude acclimatization above 12,000 feet. We arrived at Base with probably a net surplus of three to five days' acclimatization for the altitude range of 12,000 to 14,000 feet.

Rainier was a magical place for many of us as we arrived in rain, with clouds racing across the lower slopes. The great mountain with its numerous glaciers had a special meaning for many of the team who had guided there over the past years, and I felt a twinge as I entered the old Guide House and found it essentially unchanged in 25 years. The memories of my youth flooded over me that moment, yet I found myself more excited than I had been 36 years before on my first climb up the Kautz Icefall.

We left the Paradise Ranger Station in fog and downpour at 3:00 P.M. for the upper mountain, not planning a particularly difficult route, but with very heavy packs—75 to 85 pounds. When guiding, we had all carried heavy loads to Camp Muir at 10,000 feet, but seldom save in rescues had we carried much weight to the summit. I thanked the Lord I was in my best shape in years and hoped the same was true of everyone else.

At noon, a day and a half later, we reached the 14,410-foot summit of Rainier. The prolonged summer storm had ended the night before. Unusually heavy amounts of snow remained on the mountain and over the Cascade Range. It seemed more like April than July. The main crater of the great volcano was a secure, sheltered, and unusually luxurious place as we pitched several tents close to the southeast edge. It was the first time in many ascents I didn't immediately have to descend and face the routine world.

As soon as the tents were up, Gary Ullin had the expedition's Frisbee out, and thus began our accelerated acclimatization program. We had split up into tentative groups, though we had made no final determination of who would climb with whom in the U.S.S.R. Evans, Stanley, Glidden and Lev settled in one McKinley tent. Steck, Ullin, Roskelley, Marts, and Higgins were in two Eddie Bauer Himalayan tents. Schoening, Lowe, Sarnquist, and Kopczynski were in another McKinley. I was part of a fairly animated group composed of Hoey, Carson, and Williamson, all sandwiched in one Bauer Himalayan. We not only began to condition our bodies to the altitude, we began to try to understand each other.

We climbed new and old route variations, descending to the base of the climb, working our way back to our new home in the great mountain's crater. The summit of Rainier had become a familiar and friendly place. The equipment was checking out very well. Pete and I mainly worried about drying it out at the airport motel before leaving for the Soviet Union. Our concern was how much it would weigh and how much additional charge there would be for wet gear as we loaded it on an SAS plane.

Evans's group did an excellent direct and new route in the Sunset Amphitheater and Schoening and Steck took their teams on a previously climbed but fine ice route on the north edge of the amphitheater. Bruce Carson, Marty Hoey, and I were stymied by heavy rockfall on the South Tahoma Glacier headwall, and we had laboriously to retrace our steps down a very steep ice ramp that had led up to the South Tahoma and 4,000 vertical feet back up the

Tahoma Glacier to our home on the summit. As we reached 14,000 feet, the wind was working up into a major storm, and a half hour after we were back in our tent the snow began.

Given the nearby Pacific Ocean and the height of the mountain, a storm on the summit of Rainier is really the equivalent of a very high wind tunnel, as the strong southwest winds collide with the ice mass of the mountain, the moist air adiabatically cooled by 60 to 70 degrees with resultant year-round arctic cold, snow, and turbulence. We had picked the appropriate testing place. The winds roared through the camp, and a variety of activities unfolded within the tents and the somewhat luxurious combination igloo–snow cave designed and built by Evans's group. Bridge was going on in the Steck and Ullin tent; chess of a sort in the tent I shared with Marty, Bruce, and Jed; reading and occasional conversation about high-altitude illness and mountain medicine in Pete's tent; and a great deal of digging and enlarging and bragging about how comfortable they were in Evans's group's igloo.

The storm became so violent by Monday morning that we wondered whether we could get down in time to catch our plane for Moscow on Thursday. We had to get down by Wednesday evening.

The climbing had been good as a catalyst, but the storm provided an opportunity for personalities to emerge. I liked everyone in varying ways and was pleased with the way people had sorted out in strength, personality, and compatibility. I was especially drawn to Gary Ullin and almost equally to John Roskelley.

Ullin was funny, slightly cynical, though basically idealistic, and he reminded me of myself 20 years before, except that I had never learned to fly jet airliners. Roskelley was an incredibly free spirit, independent yet helpful: while the various teams did their routes, Roskelley had descended to Paradise alone in two hours to spend a few

39

hours with his wife, Joyce, and then returned to the summit in the almost unbelievable time of three hours. Nine thousand feet in three hours! He too was funny; it was an impish, wild funniness, yet I trusted him without really knowing him well.

The expedition as a whole was coming together in very reassuring ways. A spirit of easiness and friendliness, rare for such a large group, developed. In Moscow, when we selected teams for the four objectives in the Pamirs, we could not guess that the groups would fold together so amicably and climb so well with one another. Pete was especially pleased with the spirit of the group, and I merely worried that he might be slightly disillusioned to find that several of the members were not exactly the clean cutters he imagined them to be.

Early Wednesday morning, July 10, we cooked breakfast with the storm howling outside and then began to break camp. As the various members began striking tents, cleaning up the camp area, and organizing their loads in full storm, I knew we had a winning combination.

We descended in closely grouped ropes in 60- to 70-mile-per-hour winds and stinging blizzard and broke out of the cloudcap storm at about 11,800 feet, led by the old crevasse sniffer, Fred Stanley. Not many hours later, we found ourselves at our airport motel surrounded by a sea of equipment, drying tents, and sleeping bags, and gripped by an enormous appetite for milk shakes on the part of one faction and martinis on another. One small group composed of a couple of older members desired as much as they could get of both.

CHAPTER TWO

▲

The Nations Gather in Moscow

The hours closed fast on our departure on July 11 from the Seattle-Tacoma Airport for Copenhagen and Moscow. The months of preparation paid off; there were virtually no hitches as we said goodbye to loved ones and well-wishers. I especially remember the forlorn face of the poignant and beautiful Gretchen Daiber as she reluctantly released her fiancé, Gary Ullin, to join the rest of us climbing aboard the SAS 707. Equally sad were Fred Stanley's pretty blond wife and their two towheaded youngsters. They looked a bit bewildered by it all.

We had been on board the flight approximately an hour, racing northeast across Canada toward Greenland, when we learned that the attaché case containing our seven Motorola HT22 radios had been left behind at the airport. This was a hard blow, as we had had a very difficult time obtaining the radios, finally getting them through the generosity of the National Ski Patrol in Denver and largely by virtue of the efforts of Herbert Schneider, an official of that organization. The possibility of getting the radios past Soviet customs was marginal at best, and if they were to arrive after the expedition had landed, the chances they would be passed were very slim indeed. The loss was especially sad, since we were counting heavily on those versatile radios to maintain contact among the American teams and between the various teams and Base Camp.

The fantastic, surreal mountains of Greenland seemed endless as Captain Lars Lingren tried hard to get the radios located in Seattle and on their way to Moscow by the fastest connection. We suspected the effort would prove fruitless, as they would have to enter with us in order to pass Russian customs at all. Captain Lingren's efforts were fabulous, but the radios arrived a day later and a day too late. We cleared customs in Moscow without one piece of our baggage being inspected. But when the radios arrived, they were immediately and irrevocably impounded by Soviet customs. We wondered through the unusual summer whether the radios could have made any difference in the way things eventually turned out.

Landing in Moscow, green and gray on this July evening, was pure storybook for our wide-eyed entourage, mainly schooled in fairy tales and heavy assessments of Soviet life. After a brief stopover in Copenhagen, where Mike Yokell joined us, and then in Stockholm, the entry into the Soviet Union was one of deep contrast. We had flown for two hours over the endlessly flat western Russian landscape and then, descending through cloud layers into varicolored green made drab by the overcast, we got glimpses of the great city of 7,000,000 people astride the Moskva River.

As we emerged from the aircraft, we were struck by the number and variety of Soviet jet aircraft at the big airport facility and by the number of uniformed people who were on the ramp attending unloading planes. The uniforms were largely of the Red Army; the last uniforms we had seen were of SAS passenger agents and pursers, and very few of those at that. As we entered the Soviet customs deck in the terminal, there were more uniforms, mostly on young men in the smart, somehow classic and dated Soviet jackbooted uniform of the army. The thought crossed more than one of our minds that perhaps it was best that we had left the radios behind.

We were met at customs by Christopher Wren, who was fluent in Russian and totally at home in the Soviet environment. He had been training conscientiously, running cross-country ski trails during the winter and jogging Moscow running paths in the spring. He looked very fit and very much at ease as we shifted from one foot to the other under the eyes of the soldiers and customs officers. Chris introduced us to the handsome and dapper Eugene Gippenreiter, and we were suddenly convinced we were in the Soviet Union.

Eugene, who speaks excellent English, is a physiologist doing research in high-altitude metabolism, and is Secretary for International Affairs of the Soviet Federation of Mountaineering. He waited until everyone was assembled in the customs area, our group now including some Dutch climbers, and then asked that our passports be handed to a Soviet customs officer, who appeared to be of commissioned rank. Our packs and duffel bags were in a row at the customs tables, and we were simply told to pick them up and store them in the baggage chambers of two large airport buses standing by for us outside the terminal building. Gippenreiter quickly returned and handed over our stamped passports.

I can't imagine anyone other than Henry Kissinger having ever been more rapidly processed entering the Soviet Union. I told Eugene about the radios, and he made a sad face. "As you can see, it would have been done without effort; now it is hard to say. I doubt they will pass by themselves. I will arrange for you to try, assuming SAS gets the case here by tomorrow afternoon. It is too bad." I met the SAS agent, Mr. Nordburg, and we arranged to communicate later by phone. He also did not seem particularly optimistic.

We entered the city from the north, past monuments to great tank battles where the Russians had turned back the German panzers, past endless blocks of apartment buildings, what appeared to be suburbs, shopping centers, vast numbers of people taking the Friday evening air, along very wide tree-defined boulevards of considerable beauty. We were surprised to see so much traffic, and to see how fast the drivers went in this rigidly organized society.

We came to a series of what appeared to be inner-city squares, in one of which Eugene pointed out the famed Russia (pronounced Rooseeuh) Hotel, then the remote, almost fairylike yet brooding Kremlin; farther south lay our hotel. "You are staying in the Sputnik Hotel," Eugene began. "It is a hotel for sportsmen and sports delegations. It is a new structure and you will like it." By the time we reached the modest, modern Sputnik, it was clear we had traversed one of the largest cities of the world.

Checking in at the Sputnik was not exactly like arriving at the Plaza, it was more reminiscent of arrival at summer scout camp combined with freshman registration at college. We began to feel the barrier of the Russian language as we tried to cope with the system of registering, which also included the somewhat unnerving relinquishment of one's passport. "Zstrasvideyeh" (hello), "spasibo" (thank you), and "ochen horoscho" (that's okay, or everything's fine) were not nearly enough to cope with this subtle, complicated tongue; and our two qualified Russian linguists were hard pressed to get everyone sorted out and into assigned rooms.

As we arrived, others were coming in from a variety of directions and countries. The Scots pulled up in a van with "Scottish Pamirs Expedition" in supergraphic lettering across its sides, and shortly after they were followed by a slightly scruffy and seemingly cool collection of English-men who had just arrived from the Finland Station. We realized we were witnessing the arrival of part of the Who's Who in British mountaineering: Doug Scott, Paul Nunn, Tut Braithwaite, and three others reputed to be equally able though not quite as well known—Clive Row-land, Guy Lee, and Speedy Smith. The Scots included Allen North, Ronnie Richards, and Graham Tiso.

We soon realized that more than a hot English and a strong Scottish team had arrived for the Pamirs gathering. We learned from one of the Germans who had arrived ear-lier that there were two teams of fine French climbers, several of whom had done a number of the big-wall clas-sics in Europe including the Eiger north face and the Walker spur of the Grandes Jorasses in the Alps as well as the Cassin ridge on McKinley in Alaska. There were also two groups of Germans (one of which was Bavarian) who had done similar notable European and overseas climbs. There was a large and formidable group of Japanese, sev-eral with Himalayan experience.

Two groups of Austrians had arrived and were already said to be at Base Camp, a fact which made all the rest of the teams somehow uneasy. The first group, about eight experienced alpine climbers, was led by Wolfgang Axt, one of Austria's most famous mountaineers, with broad ex-perience in the Himalayas and the Alps. A second very large and unknown group of Austrians (numbering over fifty), led by Marcus Schmuck, who had been on the first ascent of Broad Peak (26,400 feet) in the Karakoram Range was also established at Base Camp.

There were unconfirmed and undetailed rumors of strong teams of Czechs, Poles, Estonians, and Siberians who would also operate out of the Achik Tash Valley along with the 160 Western European, Japanese, and American climbers. There was even the report of an all-female ex-pedition of eight of the best Soviet women climbers, who would attempt the first all-women ascent and traverse (east to west) of Peak Lenin—a formidable climb by anyone's standards.

The tension for the Americans, and we suspected for most of the others, was rising as the first evening wore on. It began to emerge that the Soviets had made various arrangements with the different national teams. This was not particularly surprising; these were, many of them, world-class climbers who certainly had not come to make a ceremonial gesture on a Soviet national shrine—that is, merely to climb a standard route on Peak Lenin. The English, for example, were to be allowed to make an attempt to one side or the other of the central buttress agreed upon as the objective of the Americans on the east face of Lenin. The Scots were to be allowed to go north beyond Peak Nineteen (more formally named the "Peak of the Nineteenth Party Congress") to a group of unclimbed peaks lying along and to the west of the Chinese border and also do a route on the east face of Peak Lenin. One group of the French had been granted permission to climb something about which no one seemed to have any clear notion save that it was south and east of Peak Lenin. Peak 6852? There was no clear indication what any of the other national groups—the Dutch, the Swiss, the Japanese, the Bavarians, and the Austrians—were specifically going to do, but it was quite clear it was going to be crowded in the Pamirs.

Apprehension enveloped many of our climbers as we sat down to dinner at a commons-like table in the Sputnik grand ballroom. The French and English seemed friendly enough, but not very communicative. They were clearly testing us, just as we endeavored to appear slightly bored in their eyes. Nevertheless, several of us began to suspect the summer might take on the characteristics of an international free-for-all rather than of a series of discrete mini-expeditions operating, as we had been led to expect, in relative isolation on new, unclimbed routes in the great Pamirs. All of the elements of mountaineering gamesmanship had begun to surface, and we found ourselves falling into the pattern, remonstrating with each other not to reveal our objectives.

Eugene Gippenreiter remained at the hotel talking with people who appeared to be officials of some sort, but who were never introduced to us. He came around after a time, apparently having heard that rumors were generating at a fierce pace. Questions from some of the more anxious American climbers led him to state categorically that the various goals agreed upon in the discussion in April between Pete Schoening and the Soviet Federation leaders would be strictly honored. He seemed somewhat hurt as he declared that Soviet mountaineers keep their word, but the apprehension grew on all sides as the rumors circulated from team to team.

When Eugene confirmed that 62 Austrians were indeed already at the Base Camp, wild visions of that huge contingent arose, of their swarming into the more remote areas beyond Peak Lenin, knocking off unclimbed summits we had vague hopes of doing. With that news, we almost immediately wondered why, if 62 Austrians could come to the U.S.S.R., was it such a task to get permission for nineteen Americans? The question was never answered, and it took on even more perplexing character as we arrived at Base and discovered just who the large second group of Austrians were.

Saturday, July 13, was our single day allotted for sightseeing and final arrangements in Moscow. Though everyone was thoroughly zonked out by jet lag, we dutifully fell in behind our tour leaders bound for the Kremlin, the Metropole, the Dollar Store, the Moscow subway, and various other sites. The day was too brief. There was so much to see and learn. If only the books on the Soviet Union and the Russians written by Robert Kaiser and Hedrick Smith had been available (they were published in 1976), we would have known better what we were seeing and passing through. Nevertheless, certain strong impressions formed in our minds. Most of these were reinforced on our return from the Pamirs when we spent another two and a half days in Moscow. Even though not very often apparent, the hand of war and the ravages of battle haunt Moscow with a bloody memory made concrete by heavy neo-classical, sometimes grand monuments. The suffering over the years must have been enormous. Figures vary, but it seems reasonably certain that more than 55 million people died in Russia and the U.S.S.R. in World Wars I and II. (This does not take into account the many who died as a result of the Revolution itself.)

The city of Moscow seems, for the most part, fastidiously clean. The subway runs efficiently to the second and has an almost surgical quality. There is no graffiti. People move about with little outward passion or zest except where small children are concerned. Many of us, the Europeans included, had expected to find the Muscovites lively, gregarious, contentious—above all, infused with a kind of urban humor about man's fate; instead, they seemed merely stolid and indifferent.

It was hard to know why the collective personality seemed so stiff and cold; individual meetings with Soviet citizens of different professional and sporting backgrounds seemed to bring the Russians' psyches back into scale. They were charming and they were curious about the reasons for our visit and they wanted very much to communicate about their own various activities and the principal qualities of Soviet life. Still, there was an essential seriousness and somberness, even among the mountaineers—those usually free spirits—for which we were not prepared. I say this not as a criticism of Russian life as such but as an observation that a collective sense of suffering seems deeply burned into their individual memories and everything they do is, therefore, somehow related to a haunted past.

By noon of our one-day tour, two of our more adventurous tourists, John Marts and John Roskelley (who had forfeited sleep the night before and spent most of the evening touring after-hours bars with a couple of Russian students), had broken off from the group in search of more offbeat photographic perspectives than our postcard itinerary offered. Word seems to travel fast, even in crowded downtown Moscow, and we soon learned that two Americans were in the process of being arrested. Actually the incident had run its course by the time we heard of it. The two Johns thought it would add a new dimension to their photographic perspective of the Soviet Union to show Soviet citizens at work, candid portraits of faces in the crowd.

As they approached the busy intersection before GUM, the large Soviet department store, they jay-walked in the middle of the block. Almost immediately an irate Russian traffic policeman was upon them, loudly berating them for failing to observe the proper intersection. At first they did not understand, but the officer by gestures finally conveyed their offense. He continued to shout at the two Johns, and a fair sized crowd gathered. The policeman seemed to be enjoying the furor, playing to his somber, curious audience; and Roskelley, sensing the theatrical aspects of the encounter for the policeman and the fact that they were being used as whipping boys, began to match shouts. John and the policeman ended nose to nose offering epithets and invectives, one for lack of hospitality and understanding, the other for the stupidity and arrogance of foreign visitors. It became comical and finally the crowd began to titter and giggle.

Through all of the encounter, Marts kept shooting photographs of the scene; and the policeman, hardly losing contact with Roskelley, kept threatening arrest for photographing a Soviet officer. Roskelley and Marts (and the rest of us, for that matter) were unaware that it is considered a crime to photograph soldiers, policemen, and astronauts (emerging from their space capsules) in the Soviet Union.

The cop appeared to be suggesting that Marts remove the film from his camera and that seemed to more deeply inflame Roskelley, who began to raise questions about freedom and the rights of the individual in the Soviet Union. A Soviet citizen came along and tried to untangle the situation. He seemed to be an academic person and was somewhat amused. He pointed out to the officer that the two Americans were obviously foreigners, probably couldn't read Russian, and were probably used to crossing streets in the middle of the block in their own country.

Pete was troubled about the incident with the policeman. Anything that threatened our hard-won relationship with the Soviets jeopardized the whole effort in his eyes. I felt a little more relaxed about things. Roskelley was definitely a hotshot, but he was also basically a good guy, a source of spirit and fire, and very steady when it was needed. The team continued to shake down. Friendships were forming, but there were still no cliques, and our two new members, Chris Wren and Mike Yokell, were folding into the group as if they had been a part of it from the beginning. If I had a worry, it was only that Pete's straightness was not fully understood by many of the climbers, especially the gifted, ultrarelaxed, irreverent souls who comprised over two-thirds of the group.

When we got to the Sputnik, Pete and I sat in a corner by ourselves and discussed climbing teams and objectives in the Pamirs. We were more convinced than ever that we had four of the best objectives, probably *the* four best targets of the summer. The fancy brochure of the Soviet International Camp that had suddenly appeared as we arrived in Moscow gave us a pretty vivid sense of what lay ahead. We only wished the Soviets could have made such material available earlier.

Pete had in his mind a very clear picture of how each of the four teams would shape up. I really found nothing to dispute, but I was surprised at Pete's view of my own involvement. John Evans would lead the largest and perhaps the strongest team to do the very difficult, dangerous, and unclimbed central buttress of the east face of Peak Lenin. The team would be composed of Evans, Bruce Carson, Peter Lev, Jeff Lowe, Fred Stanley, and Al Steck.

Jock Glidden would lead a group of five to the unclimbed and challenging east face of Peak 6852 (22,480 feet). If they had enough steam after that climb, they would do Lenin by one of the ordinary routes. Glidden's team was made up of Molly Higgins, Jed Williamson, Chris Wren, and Mike Yokell.

Pete would lead the exploratory effort to the peaks of the Dzerschinsky Glacier area, which lay to the southwest of the Lenin massif. This would be the only American team to visit totally unexplored terrain, which reputedly included some first-class summits along the Dzerschinsky Glacier. In Pete's team were Marty Hoey, Chris Kopczynski, and Frank Sarnquist.

In groups such as we had put together, almost any one person could assume the leadership role, and, in fact, many decisions were taken by team consensus. I had seen myself in the overall operation as an old expedition hand, as a facilitator and, I hoped, a relatively low-profile alter ego to Pete. I was surprised, therefore, to discover that Pete felt I should lead the strong team of Marts, Roskelley, and Ullin to do the north face of Peak Nineteen (19,423 feet). As it turned out, the tasks of leadership tended to divide themselves equally among the four of us.

We would follow Peak Nineteen with an ascent of the east face of Lenin, though probably not on a route as extreme as that which confronted John Evans's group. All that promised a very full summer indeed.

We called Mr. Nordburg at SAS late Saturday afternoon and were informed that Soviet customs did not intend to release the radios to us, and that there was just nothing that could be done about the situation. Eugene Gippenreiter was back at the Sputnik helping everyone get organized for departure, and he assured us the Soviet Federation would provide each team with a radio capable of communicating with Base Camp.

By Saturday evening, we could think of nothing but the Pamirs. The thought of our hard-won acclimatization's wearing off with each hour spent at sea level in Moscow fueled an irrational impatience. We had been down from 14,000 feet only three days, and by the next afternoon we would be back at 11,700 feet in the Achik Tash Valley. Some of us were more relieved to be leaving not because we were so concerned about acclimatization but because we honestly felt another night on the town would surely yield some kind of incident which might well delay the whole expedition.

On July 13, an hour's drive out of the suburbs into the darkened countryside south of Moscow, marked by what appeared to be occasional military checkpoints, brought us to the airport, a fairly modern and heavily used terminal which apparently serves exclusively for flights to the interior cities of the Soviet Union. We arrived at 9:00 P.M., just at dusk.

We were told we would depart in about 45 to 90 minutes. The flight to Osh, the capital of the Kirghiz Soviet Socialist Republic, about 2,700 miles to the southeast, would take about seven hours in a four-engined Ilyushin turboprop, flying at about 400 miles an hour. There might be one stop enroute at the city of Aktyubinsk in Kazakhstan, at the south end of the Ural Mountains. Two affable, rather modishly attired young men, Valody and Mishka, took over as we arrived and seemed to have the task of providing liaison between Aeroflot and the Soviet Federation of Mountaineering.

The amount of baggage for over 100 mountaineers was pretty awesome. We had tried to hold the total baggage weight per member of the U.S. team to around 50 pounds, inclusive of all personal and individual gear, and had another 3,000 pounds in food, tentage, stoves, climbing gear, and hardware. Somehow, on the average, we seemed lighter than the other groups.

Valody and Mishka circulated between the aircraft being loaded with the climbers' gear and the waiting lounge, which had taken on the character of a mid-1930s movie about the Orient Express or the last train for Peking. There were exotic-hatted Uzbekistanis, Mongolian-looking Kirghiz in even more remarkable hats, long-haired Americans and Japanese, longer-haired Englishmen from Nottinghamshire, several shy Dutchmen with two rather pretty Dutch women, heavily accented but somewhat taciturn Scots, a group of seemingly diffident, slightly jaded Frenchmen, and two friendly, cheery teams of Germans. The Bavarian group was also distinguished by a very pretty woman who later turned out to be a model and a skillful climber as well.

The evening became a kaleidoscope of events, impressions, and frustrations. The aircraft was partly loaded when the captain halted the storing of luggage. He suspected there was fuel in some of the stoves of the climbing teams. The search of the baggage revealed there was indeed fuel in the tanks of the stoves of the Dutch, Bavarians, and the Japanese. All equipment would be checked to the satisfaction of the plane commander. Hours more delay. Marts had the only alternative: we must ensure that the American expedition equipment made it on the flight. The only sure way was to have Valody and Mishka come to our aid. Since we had been counseled that the Soviet citizens were largely above bribery, we decided we must appeal to friendship. Accordingly, we purchased three bottles of quite good Georgian champagne at the canteen adjacent to the lounge and invited Valody and Mishka to join us in celebrating Soviet-American understanding. This they did with enthusiasm, one or the other leaving the table periodically to check in at the loading area.

Slowly but quite clearly we made our point. After two

hours (and two more bottles of champagne) in which Marts, Ullin, Lowe, Roskelley, Steck, and I quietly established bonds with the two young Russians, we began to receive assurance the gear would go aboard the plane with us. The plane *was* loaded again, but we suspected the baggage was being taken through the cargo port on one side and out the other, a suspicion strengthened by a new rumor which maintained that the plane was taking on an unusually heavy load of fuel and would not stop enroute to Osh.

The English and Scots joined in the drinking with the Americans, and the original objective of ensuring that the expedition gear got on board the plane appeared to be vanishing. Meanwhile, Pete Schoening and Chris Wren maintained a steady presence in the loading area and were probably most responsible for the gear's getting stowed safely aboard. It all came to naught in Osh the next day as we transferred to smaller aircraft for the flight to Daraut Kurgan. The American expedition gear and that of several other teams was not loaded and was brought over to Base Camp by trucks the next day. As it turned out, the loss in time was not as great as we had imagined, and it proved we were simply a bit overanxious. It can be fairly stated that the presence of over twelve national climbing teams, of whom 62 people were a group of Austrians we hadn't seen but who were already in Base, put each of us in a very nervous frame of mind.

We finally boarded the plane in Moscow at about 1:30 A.M., exhausted and feeling very little pain from a substantial amount of champagne and brandy. There is probably no more euphoric or exciting group experience than being in an expedition in the final stages of its approach to distant high mountains. Tomorrow we would see the Pamirs! Even at that late hour and with the continuing effects of jet lag, the sense of shared expectation and anticipation was electric.

The Ilyushin was a noisy aircraft, resembling very much

the somewhat smaller Vickers Viscount. The craft lumbered, heavily laden, down what seemed an endless runway, and then we were airborne, climbing to what must have been 26,000 feet or so judging by the lack of definition of the ground. The Ilyushin rattled along hour after hour across the vastness of the Soviet Union that can only be measured in time, in endless hundreds of miles per hour, southeast across the steppe, flying high enough for nothing below to be distinguishable, low enough in the moonlit night to hint that there was nothing much below which could be distinguished. Gary, the seasoned airline pilot, was slightly uneasy about the amount of vibration in the aircraft, a concern which was immediately translated into consumption of a bottle of Scotch I was saving for special occasions at Base Camp.

During the flight and a bit earlier in the terminal it had become apparent that a romance had descended upon our disparate band. Gary, John Roskelley, and I had, in a brotherly, playful way, over the past week and a half become quite close to Marty. Whatever the apparent implications of our propositions and libidinous suggestions, it was a friendship based on laughter and shared experience. For it to be anything more in the context of our expedition composed of seventeen men and two women was seen to be impractical if not undesirable. As we saw that Marty and Pete Lev had drawn apart from the Americans in the plane, we realized that the romance several of us had personally sought to avoid was there and probably unpreventable.

Successful group dynamics in an expedition of carefully selected, potentially compatible climbers is a difficult enough achievement under the best of circumstances. Altitude, duration of the operation, homesickness, personality differences, and illness all take their toll; and it is clear that the welding of a harmonious, homogeneous team takes constant individual effort. A number of us saw the introduction of a romantic component into the expedition as a distraction and a diversion from the goal of cohesiveness.

It was our concern for the overall chemistry of the expedition that aroused our apprehension, not the fact of a relationship for Marty and Peter, both of whom we liked.

The night seemed endless as the Ilyushin rattled along and we played a moderately successful game of liar's dice with the English, and finally the sleep of exhaustion overtook us. We were awakened by the *ohs* and *ahs* of fellow passengers as the Tien Shan Range and the northern Pamirs loomed in the east on the left side of the aircraft. It was a very impressive sight, for the whole of the range as far as the eye could see seemed resplendently clear and blindingly white.

The whiteness is what is so particularly striking about the Pamirs. They are almost covered in a glacial mantle with few exposed rock walls or faces. The summits of the Pamirs are not characterized on the average by the sharp, pronounced peaks one finds to the south in the Hindu Kush Range or to the south and east in the Karakoram. Massive long ice ridges with cascading, hanging glaciers on the flanks are more often the rule.

The Pamirs are at the intersection points of four of the world's highest mountain ranges: the Tien Shan to the northeast, the Kunlun to the east, the Hindu Kush to the south, and the Karakoram to the southeast. The Pamirs plateau maintains an average height above 10,000 feet, save in the south, where it drops to about 8,000 feet. The bulk of the range rises as impressively above its base as almost any part of the trans-Himalayan system—often 12,000–13,000 feet. The highest summits in the Soviet Pamirs are Peak of Communism, 24,590 feet, and Peak Lenin, 23,406 feet, and there are a great many peaks above 21,000 feet, a substantial number of which have not been climbed. The highest peak in the entire Pamirs is Kungar (25,325 feet), which is found in China, north and east of the Lenin Massif. Several of the largest glaciers in Asia are formed in the Pamirs, and many of the great rivers of central Asia originate in its vast watersheds. The Markan-Sou and Gez flow eastward to form the Kashgar Darya River in China. The Vakhan Darya provides the southern boundary of the Pamirs and becomes, with the Garma Chesmon, the Gcount, and the Bartang, the great Amu Darya River. In the northwest, the Morik-Sou and Kzyl-Sou form the Vakhsh, which traverses the whole of Tadjikistan from northwest to the southwest, and then flows into the Pandj before it becomes the Amu Darya.

The Pamirs are a young range geologically. In the late Tertiary Period, they were lifted up in the folding of the earth's crust from an ocean bed that extended from the Caspian Sea to the edge of the Mongolian Desert. Later, during the Pleistocene Epoch, extensive ice masses covered the entire Pamirs region, and today large glaciers still lie above 12,000 feet in the range.

Landing at Osh, an ancient trade center on the Chinese caravan route, we found ourselves letting down from the dazzling panorama of a seemingly unbroken range of ice into a land of opposites. Osh, a city founded in A.D. 500, lies near the foot of the frontal ranges of the Pamirs, and is a very significant agricultural center as well as the center for the substantial Soviet military forces guarding that part of the Sino-Soviet frontier. At 4,000 feet above sea level, this part of Kirghizia is very arid but fertile, and large-scale irrigation is evident.

What makes great mountains so fascinating to everyone, not just to climbers, is the strange juxtapositions within which they are found: the Saint Elias Range rises literally out of the sea to over 18,000 feet; K2 rises from one of the great desert areas of the world to 28,250 feet; Everest at 29,028 feet has one foot in the jungles of Nepal and the other in barren upland wastes of Tibet; Mount Kenya is an equatorial phenomenon of glaciers joining tropical forest in the most unlikely heart of Africa; and the Pamirs generate some of the largest and longest glaciers in Asia bordered by several of the most arid areas in the world.

As we debarked, uniformed Kirghiz schoolchildren met

us at the ramp leading into the terminal and presented bouquets of flowers. A delegation of business-suited Kirghiz, looking as if they had left their ponies and Tamerlane on the outskirts of town, greeted us with warm dignity. We were ushered through the pleasant, modern, well-lighted terminal to a second-floor dining area where we were served a delicious meal by a group of predominantly European-looking women. Somehow, we got the vague impression they were part of the Soviet Ladies Aid Society or some equivalent. They were much friendlier than anyone who served us in Moscow. Michael Monastyrski, the commandant of the Pamirs camp, speaking in English, offered words of greeting to the assembled climbers, saying the Soviets were pleased and excited by the prospect of the greatest gathering of international mountaineering teams in climbing history.

Our schedule was tight following the delay in Moscow, and we were quickly reloaded into a fleet of four Yak 40s, a kind of mini-Boeing 727, each carrying about thirty passengers. We had seen a wide variety of Soviet jets in Moscow at both airports, many of them advanced-looking in design, but the Yak 40s were by far the most appealing. As we boarded our particular aircraft, the Americans assigned to three planes, we were treated to a glimpse of our first really attractive Soviet stewardess, and by the skeptical look on Michael Monastyrski's face, I knew a glimpse would be all we would have.

As we took off for Daraut Kurgan, the new, unlikely, contrasting world of the Pamirs unfolded. We leveled out over the Alai Mountains, a respectable range rising to 16,000 feet with numerous small glaciers and permanent snowfields. Cameras began clicking, the government's admonition against photography in certain places having been forgotten in the excitement of discovery. The pretty stewardess conscientiously reminded the passengers of their obligations. Monastyrski said it succinctly: "My friends, we are very close to our real world. The Soviet government appreciates you do not photograph from aircraft. I appreciate personally." We already knew we liked Monastyrski, and the cameras disappeared immediately.

The Pamirs were now visible in much clearer, more intimate detail. The highest points, Peak of Communism (formerly Mount Stalin) and Peak Lenin, defined the most immediate parts of the range, though the Pamirs are a much more complex and extensive body of mountains than most realize, and the best, most challenging peaks lie in the remote in-between and beyond from Lenin and Communism. Farther to the north and east and in China, the great mass of Kungur bulked on the horizon. We knew the more distant peaks, however appealing, were beyond our reach, but we also knew the east face of Peak Lenin, Peak 6852, Peak Nineteen, and the summits along the Dzerschinsky Glacier were more than adequate objectives. As we flew on toward Daraut Kurgan, the mountains along the Dzerschinsky Glacier area southwest of Lenin, where Pete Schoening's group would go, came into view. Peak Nineteen sheered to the left of Lenin and looked like it would take a good part of a summer itself. We could not see the east faces of Lenin and 6852, as we were approaching from the north and west, but we had one Austrian photograph (our only good photo of the Pamirs) that revealed the substantial difficulties of Lenin's east buttress and the unclimbed east side of Peak 6852.

We landed at Daraut Kurgan—a very old fortress town built originally by Kohkand warriors of antiquity, with a dusty, unpaved airstrip, but capable of handling sophisticated jet aircraft—and knew immediately as we disembarked that we were in the heart of Asia. Daraut Kurgan goes back to the Silk Route days of the tenth century, and the succeeding mud brick fortresses built on the ruins of one another defended traders and local inhabitants against marauding nomads who swept down the Alai Valley from the east. There were Kirghiz officials in suits without ties and Soviet officials in suits with ties, but there were also the authentic silent Kirghiz in mixed European and Central Asian dress, and a few in completely Kirghiz attire, and one was reminded of American Indians at Bureau of Land Management meetings where the native people looked embarrassed on their own land. The incredible recent mechanization and modernization of a very old and mysterious land reminded us somehow of the settling of the western United States. The principal difference seems to be that the native people remain the most numerous in Kirghizia.

We received the greetings of Michael Anufrikov, the Secretary General of the Soviet Federation of Mountaineering, as we awaited the unloading of personal gear from the Yak. Anufrikov was very formal, made a perfunctory tribute to the great Socialist Republic of Kirghizia and the Kirghiz people, and welcomed us to the Pamirs. We clapped politely in appreciation; the assembled Kirghiz, some of whom might not have understood Russian, did not applaud particularly, but they smiled shyly as we looked at them. The personal baggage did not arrive on any of the flights into Daraut Kurgan. We had only our personal carry-on bags—shaving kits, stationery, extra sweaters—and as we loaded into four military trucks, we suspected it might be a long night.

We left Daraut Kurgan in our caravan of trucks with hard, rigid benches in rows athwart the rear of the vehicles. A race seemed to be on between the drivers. The dust was incredible, and we cheered our man on to take the lead and save us from suffocation. Everyone crawled out from under the truck canopy for a view.

The Pamirs were now overhead: massive ridges and faces fronted with ice, appearing horribly exposed to avalanches. We'd skirt those—somehow. The ice ridges appeared to offer escape. There was even less rock than we noted when we were flying into Osh and Daraut; the almost total mantle of ice was more dazzling than any range any of us had ever seen. There was nothing but whiteness bordered by disappearing miles of rolling grassland. And the trucks began to climb up, across the fronts of ancient moraines, the drivers now clearly racing one another on alternate tracks up the river beds of massive glacier valleys.

Although the glaciers and snowfields were not far off, the growth of mountain grass was most impressive. Even as we climbed out of the main Alai Valley, there appeared to be experimental grain plots at about the 9,000-foot level. The seedlings looked reasonably strong though thinly spread, and one could not help wondering about the first frost. Judging by the snow low down on the main peaks, the last frost in the valley could not have been long before, and September was only six weeks away. The country is reminiscent of parts of Wyoming and Colorado—perhaps also Idaho around Challis. There is a vital difference: there are no trees in the Alai Valley. The native grasses are sturdy and fairly lush between 9,000 and 12,500 feet. We had never seen such a vast grazing area.

We began to see assorted livestock as we climbed in the Achik Tash Valley, a feeder watershed of the main Alai Valley, fed by the Lenin Glacier. There was a preponderance of sheep, some goats, smaller herds of range cattle, and quite a few small herds of horses. The horses appeared to be of taller stock than the Central Asian ponies we had read about. The Soviets are introducing modern breeding programs into many lines of livestock, and these remote herds reflected this effort.

The dwellings of the nomadic Kirghiz shepherds began to appear in clusters of two, three, and four. Domelike goatskin huts built on impressively sturdy structural frameworks of interlocking wooden struts, the yurts of the Kirghiz can be erected in less than an hour and are strong enough to endure the fury of a full mountain storm. They are quite sophisticated structures, augmented by butane or

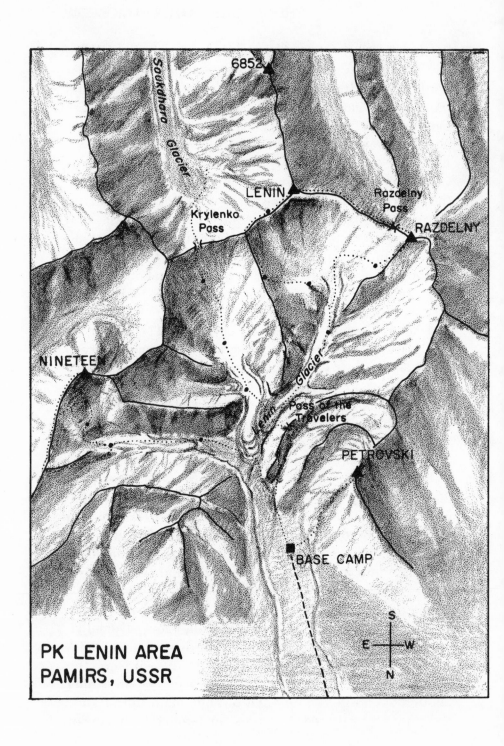

6852

Saukdhara Glacier

LENIN

Krylenko
Pass

Razdelny
Pass

RAZDELNY

NINETEEN

Lenin Glacier

Pass of the
Travelers

PETROVSKI

BASE CAMP

S
E — W
N

PK LENIN AREA
PAMIRS, USSR

propane stoves and lined inside by intricately designed colorful Kirghiz rugs, with layers of goat-wool blankets piled in corners to be used against the cold.

The people—the herdsmen, the women, the children— were fiercely, wonderfully Central Asian, their faces taken from some highly stylized early Chinese painting. Their dress was simple, functional, and quietly colorful. Their hats are especially distinctive. Wide brimmed, high crowned, subtly embroidered, they provide shade and considerable protection from the cold and wind.

As we crossed a swale, two camels suddenly loomed on the horizon against the backdrop of hanging ice, and I thought at the moment, This has got to be the ultimate scene in high-mountain travel: camels and glaciers! We began to encounter a series of small, clear, deep lakes in various levelings of the moraine benches. There had to be spirit people in those lakes. The setting was too perfect for there not to be. The almost haunted quality of this ancient place had begun to work its spell on us. We came to wonder more about spells and spirits as the summer wore on.

The ancient people of the Pamirs, Hindu Kush, and Karakoram lived in a world heavily peopled with spirits of all kinds. In spite of the advent of Islam in the relatively recent history of these more remote valleys, and the essentially areligious Soviet philosophy of the last 40 to 50 years, a good deal of spirit belief and superstition still persists.

A final rise and we leveled out in a wide grassy meadow. The Soviet International Camp, with its row of high flagpoles set in the center of a quadrangle and the orderly rows of tents, was abruptly before us. We were in the heart of the Achik Tash (place of waters and wind), a place the Soviets call the "Valley of the Edelweiss."

CHAPTER THREE

▲

Base Camp under the "Roof of the World"

By the time we reached Base Camp on July 14, we were not terribly surprised at the nature of the elaborate installation. Having seen the four-color brochures describing the Pamirs Camp on our arrival in Moscow, we again wondered why the only photographs Pete Schoening had been able to obtain in Moscow on his visit in April had been those four grainy, blurred black and white shots that appeared to have been taken in the late 1890s or early 1900s. Now seeing the real thing, it definitely seemed that the Russians might have feared the Americans would not take part in such a highly organized and, in a sense, regimented and populous international camp that offered, as it turned out (but not revealed in advance), a relatively narrow range of objectives for the very large numbers of assembled climbers.

In fairness, it should be said that the Russians tried very hard to fulfill the promises to the Americans of whatever objectives were requested. The climbing goals which were agreed upon for our teams were very good ones; and had the summer gone at all normally, we probably would have returned with several outstanding mountaineering achievements to our credit. But on our arrival at Base, the sense of a true expeditionary experience was for the moment lost in the mechanized bustle of the camp, and in the lack of intimacy afforded by over 150 persons of at least twelve different nationalities milling around and speaking in often unrecognizable tongues. Fascinating, but a bit unnerving, it was Babel among the glaciers.

We had been in camp very few minutes when we realized there was little we could do organizationally without the main bulk of our equipment to unpack and distribute. Damn Aeroflot! Most of us had our personal climbing gear such as boots and ice axes, but there were no ropes, no hardware, and no rations.

History-conscious and curious, almost all of the Americans were eager to visit the Kirghiz encampments. We strolled down in small groups through the rolling flower-strewn meadows of the old moraine, sometimes on the truck road, sometimes on footpaths. Animals were grazing everywhere. There were large flocks of sheep, goat herds, and horses and cattle in smaller numbers. We saw the camels again. They looked ridiculous but grand against the backdrop of icy ridges. And everywhere we saw incredible fields of edelweiss, the lovely off-white velvety star-shaped high-mountain flower that is regarded as almost a religious object by the mountain people of Europe.

The first yurt we came upon had several small, roly-poly, apple-cheeked Kirghiz children playing around the entrance; an older sister was acting as nursemaid. Older women momentarily poked their heads out of the entrance to the yurt, then shyly withdrew. An imposing man, apparently the head of the family, left a makeshift horse corral and walked up to us. He was fiercely elegant with the remarkably high cheekbones of the Kirghiz, a face that tapered down to a strong long chin, framed on either side by slender drooping mustaches. We offered the children chewing gum—perhaps an odd thing to give to these simple, healthy people (although we discovered later that they knew and loved gum and candy)—and presented an American expedition button to the father and herdsman.

The Kirghiz was clearly pleased and invited us to join him in a repast. He clapped his hands, and the women scurried about getting pots of some fluid and loaves of bread together. The children seemed transfixed with curiosity, and I wondered whether they had any idea of how far we had come to visit their strange and beautiful land.

In the pots we soon discovered was a grayish white substance of rather thin consistency that is in a way the national beverage of Kirghizia: fermented mare's milk. It is called "kumiss" and is said to be the main source of strength of the Kirghiz. It has a slightly sharp, slightly sour flavor; and when a bowl is offered to a guest, it is poor form not to completely consume what is put before one. None of us ever grew to like kumiss, but on the first occasion of tasting it, Pete Schoening, John Marts, and I made a brave try and actually consumed a bowl and a half before we left the yurt. Within a day both of the others were quite ill with nausea and diarrhea—Marts afflicted with this on top of the last stages of the flu he had contracted in the States. For some reason, on that occasion I was spared and developed no illness.

The Soviets were enormously proud of their mountaineering installation, and they deserve credit for their achievement in organization, logistical support, and comfort within about a mile and a half of one of the larger Central Asian glacial systems. The camp was organized along somewhat military lines, with an outer perimeter of tents, specific segments of which were assigned to various nationalities. The Americans, for example, had tents occupying the southeast corner of the camp, and were joined on the west by the Bavarians and on the north by the English and the Scots, followed by the French and the Japanese, a second group of French (Les Grenoblois), and finally another group of Germans. Opposite, and forming virtually the entire west wall of the tent compound, except for a smaller contingent of six or seven Swiss, was the Austrian contingent. Beyond the Austrians on the west and stretching around to the north were the Polish-made tents of the Soviet staff as well as the mess tent and the movie theater tent. Beyond the cookhouse and across a spring-fed creek was another smaller encampment of tents housing Siberians, Estonians, Poles, and the Soviet women's climbing team.

We learned that in addition to the Soviet women's team and all the other climbing teams at Base, another women's team had formed, composed of two Swiss, Heidi Ludi and Eva Eissenschmidt, one German lady named Margaret (whose last name we never learned), and an American, Arlene Blum. They called themselves the International Women's Team and would try the standard route on Lenin.

The Austrians were really two groups—a small experienced and more friendly contingent led by the internationally known Wolfgang Axt, and a second, hard to define, and not very friendly group of people who could not exactly be described as seasoned mountaineers. These were the "mystery Austrians" whom we had heard about in Moscow. This group was led by Marcus Schmuck, an Austrian expeditionary climber of past years, and who, it turned out, was a travel tour leader. His group of fifty "Austrian climbers" was in fact a relatively inexperienced collection of Austrian "valley walkers." He had actually brought a tour group to the Pamirs!

As we arrived in Base, we got the impression the Austrians had been there for an extended time. Although they actually arrived only two to three days ahead of us, they looked thoroughly settled in and seemed to have appropriated all the scrap wood in the camp for building benches and tables outside their tents. In sheer numbers the Austrians dominated the entire camp. Schmuck's group totaled 53 and Axt's numbered six more. It was only as we gathered for dinner the first night that we realized the meaning of organized power.

The Austrians, having arrived in Base Camp first, had established the right of being served first. The Russian camp authorities had politely (and not without a sense of embarrassment) informed the new arrivals that they would form the "second sitting" for meals in the mess tent. This arrangement worked reasonably well from the outset, largely because of the surprising lack of traditional rule breaking and individualism on the part of the fairly sizable number of British, French, and American climbers. Somehow, our Soviet hosts inspired a rare degree of tact and courtesy among these normally iconoclastic climbers. Nonetheless, Schmuck's Austrians felt compelled to demonstrate their solidarity, marching phalanxlike to the mess tent for each meal. Woe betide the hapless outsider who, having confused his schedule, tried to breach their ranks in the food line! From the very beginning Base Camp presented the aspect of a misplaced Hollywood movie set.

The food was plentiful, nourishing, and served by a kitchen staff who were a mixture of Russians and Kirghiz. The staff were almost uniformly cheerful and helpful despite the language barrier. They seemed to appreciate even the least attempt at the Russian language made by various members of the different national teams. We dined at tables of varying capacity; and while there was a tendency for the national groups to band together at mealtime, the Americans from the beginning began to have friendly exchanges with the various European teams.

Basically, the strongest and deepest bonds between the Americans and members of other groups seemed to involve five of the Englishmen, four of the Parisians, and four of the French climbers from Grenoble. Friendships also developed with a number of the German climbers.

BASE CAMP UNDER THE "ROOF OF THE WORLD"

The Russians we got to know became friends on a separate though no less significant level. In the case of outstanding Soviet mountaineers such as Kostya Kletso, Oleg Borosinek, and Vitaly Abalakov, the understanding and feeling of friendship came out of a sense of respect and an intuitive sense of just plain liking that transcended national styles and philosophies and especially the very considerable language barriers.

The friendships with Michael Monastyrski and Eugene Gippenreiter were of a different order. Their command of English (especially Gippenreiter's) made coherent exchange very easy. Gippenreiter, though very fluent and a man of rather broad interests, was a somewhat shy and quite formal person. There was, until the very last days, a distinct but unintended sense of distance about Eugene. Monastyrski, on the other hand, though not as fluent as one or two of the other Russians, thought in English. He was a remarkable combination of a man of action, an able but unobtrusive administrator, and a thoughtful, almost poetic spirit. He was knowledgeable about Shakespeare, Longfellow, and Poe, and had a distinct feeling for the elegance and density of poetry. He was the foreign person with whom I became closest.

These relationships grew through a series of tragedies that seemed to proceed from and grow on one another and in which our new friends, as well as our various American selves, played central parts. Out of these came the shared experience of rescue and failure, of risk and death, and the disturbing realization that we had experienced a season in high mountains that had essentially gotten beyond our control.

On July 15, the first morning after arrival in Base, Gary, Marty, and I got under way at 5:00 A.M. to climb a peak (Petrovski) to the southwest of Base Camp. We hadn't solved the problem of negotiating food supplies from the Soviet commissary, and our American rations had not yet arrived, so we had no breakfast. Because of my instant-demand metabolism, I wondered how long I would last on our climb of the 15,900-foot peak. Base Camp was at 11,700 feet, which meant a climb of some 4,200 feet on no nourishment at all.

In all the confusion of Base Camp and the preparations of the four American teams to get under way, it seemed clear that some effort was needed to maintain the acclimatization and physical conditioning we had earned on Rainier and in the preceding weeks of strenuous training. Various members of the team had different programs. Roskelley decided to wander cross-country, visiting the Kirghiz—people who, like him, seemed to have a special sense of freedom. Others planned to organize food and equipment; still others to walk up to the Pass of the Travelers to assess the Krylenko face.

From the northeast, Peak Petrovski offers no particular difficulty, but the north face provides a very pleasant, steep, and fairly continuous snow and ice climb. Because we had not eaten any breakfast on the morning we decided to go up, we determined to do the easy route and simply settled for conditioning and acclimatization. Besides, we had no climbing rope. Some of the Bavarians got off ahead of us and, apparently better fed and with equipment including ice screws in hand, tried the north face.

As we reached the ridge above Base, we noticed all kinds of figures emerging along the escarpments of the peak. Bruce Carson in Adidas shoes and shorts seemed to be doing some sort of rock ballet on the very questionable outcrops of near rubble. We passed a group of women and noted that the Swiss Eva Eissenschmidt did not seem to be feeling good. The Bavarians up on the ice face were using a two-man simultaneous technique, with one middleman belayer bringing up two climbers at a time and continuing the double belay as they leapfrogged over him on up the north face.

We proceeded on up toward the summit, feeling no

small amount of weakness due to lack of food, crossed a modestly exposed ice traverse, and then plodded on toward the summit. We arrived in a cloud a short while before the Bavarians. Our German friends were very cheerful, perhaps because they seemed to have rucksacks brimming with food. The Bavarians immediately seemed to sense our predicament, realized that we were without rations, and instantly offered us everything they had in what was one of the more genuinely touching moments of the summer.

We were terribly keyed up and excited about being in the great Russian mountains. From time to time the clouds had parted as we had ascended and we got glimpses of the mountains ahead and were very impressed. The north face of Peak Nineteen looked formidable.

As we arrived back in Base, cavorting down a 1,500-foot scree gully, half glissading, half bounding, feeling strong conditioning in our bodies despite the breakfastless ascent, we discovered that the native food of the day before had begun to take its toll. Several Americans were feeling very queasy, and Pete Schoening and John Evans were downright sick. Fermented mare's milk had to be the cause, at least in Pete's case, and protocol seemed a high price to pay. John and Pete had fevers, diarrhea, and nausea; the rest merely looked slightly green.

A banquet had been planned for the leaders of the international climbing teams. It was to be presented in one of the yurts a mile or so below Base. Pete couldn't take part, and I remember wishing all the Americans weren't required to go, as I had also heard rumors that guests were required to drink great bowls of the now dreaded mare's milk as well as vast amounts of assorted alcohols. Faced with drinking a lion's share of the fermented milk, I visualized myself as a permanent victim of amoebic dysentery.

Trucks hauled the widely different collection of men to the banquet. Most of the groups seemed to be represented.

71

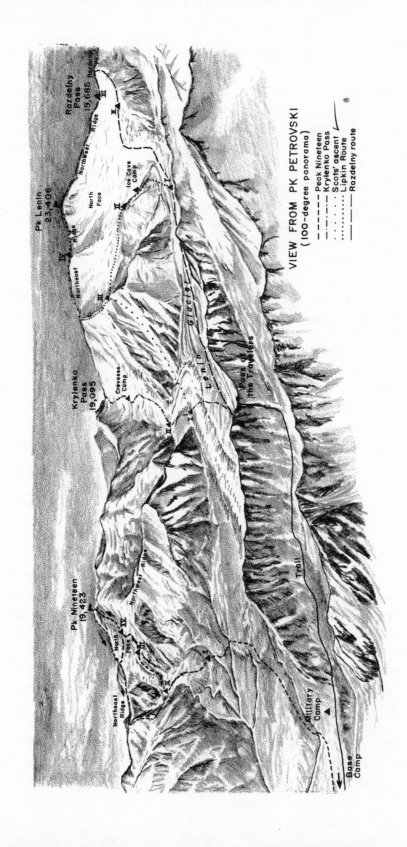

Pk Lenin
23,406

Razdelny Pass
19,685

Razdelny

Northwest Ridge

North Face

Northeast Ridge

Ridge

IV

III

II

I

Ice Cave Camp

Krylenko Pass
19,095

Crevasse Camp

II

Lenin Glacier

Pass of the Travellers

Pk Nineteen
19,423

Northeast Ridge

North Face

Northeast Ridge

II

III

II

Trail

Military Camp

Base Camp

VIEW FROM PK PETROVSKI
(100-degree panorama)

– – – – Peak Nineteen
— — — Krylenko Pass
· · · · · · · Scotts' ascent
· · · · · · · · Lipkin Route
———— Razdelny route

The exceptions included the English, who couldn't decide who their leader was; the Soviet women; the Poles; and the Siberians. The latter groups were domiciled in a camp across the stream from main Base and underneath a memorial to several dead Soviet climbers. We wondered at the time whether there might be some kind of double standard in operation for Soviet and satellite climbers, but this never really became clear.

We milled about the entrance to the yurt, admiring the thin band of geometric abstractions that formed a decorative frieze around the upper third of the tent structure. Kirghiz children peered wide-eyed around corners, taking in the array of strangers, who varied from Japanese to blond, blue-eyed Northern Europeans. Climbing boots and camp shoes were left outside, and we filtered into a spacious interior, roomy because of the truly free geodesic space afforded by the strong lattice framework on which the outer shell of hairless skins is hung.

The floor of the yurt was covered by a series of carpets about five feet wide by eight feet long. The rugs are woven by Kirghiz women and are characterized by slightly subdued vegetable-dyed colors and intricate geometric designs. Blankets made from goat wool were in piles around the perimeter of the yurt. The master of the house turned out to be a mistress, a relatively tall, stately woman with an elegantly sculpted face, with characteristic high cheekbones, a very straight nose, and a strong, well-formed mouth. She seemed to fancy me somewhat, and it was only after I had made several toasts to our hostess later in the evening that a potentially dangerous situation developed. I was not to learn of the circumstances until the next morning. It turned out my naive toasts and compliments took on the character of some kind of proposal; and egged on by some of the Kirghiz and Russian men, the handsome widow began to make plans of her own.

From the beginning, the banquet had a certain sense of

disaster about it as we noted simultaneously the very large bowls of kumiss and what appeared to be endless supplies of vodka. The mare's milk began to pass around the circle of climbers facing inward from the back of the tent. People pretended to take large, long draughts and then handed the bowl on, not having decreased its volume by more than one or two cc's. The flavor was again strong and astringent, reminding some of us on this second occasion more of sour cow's milk than anything else.

The vodka began to flow, erasing the taste of the bitter milk, and then course upon course of delicious lamb and vegetables. Then champagne of a very respectable quality (apparently from Soviet Georgia) and then, as the Russians began to toast their visitors in earnest, Kirghiz brandy. Finally there was more vodka. Memory and recollection were rapidly superseded by a vague sense of well-being in a sea of smiling faces. Kirghiz and Russian songs were sung by our hosts. Unbelievable amounts of champagne, vodka, and brandy flowed—all at 11,000 feet, where an ounce of alcohol has almost three times the effect it has at sea level. Finally, Allen North, a Scottish physician, stood up on uncertain legs and too few toes (he had lost most of his left foot in the Hindu Kush) and proposed the group sing "the song closest to the hearts of mountaineers everywhere— 'La Montanara.' " I was touched—here was a truly international gathering of climbers in the unlikely, staggeringly beautiful setting of the Pamirs, and now we were singing my favorite song. I sang out strongly the only song I know in its entirety in Italian so that at the end, one of the Italians, eyes glistening, pressed my arm and said, "Molto bello, bambino!"

The hangover the next morning from the overenthusiastic international indulgence at the yurt had a surreal quality. At around 7:00 A.M., a large herd of horses thundered past our tent, practically uprooting our tent stakes on the back side. Michael Monastyrski came by shortly after and said the Kirghiz lady of the night before was merely displaying her dowry. He chuckled and walked away. There was a persistent rumor at breakfast, a meal I could merely observe, not eat, that one of the celebrants had fallen out of the back of the truck and into the road. The understanding solicited by several of the Europeans and outright enthusiasm and friendliness of all of the Russians served to convince me that I was somehow involved in that questionable episode. We had been warned that the Russians took delight in drinking their guests under the table—in this case the carpet. What we didn't recognize was that the Russians used persons other than climbers—that is, "professionals"—to lead in the drinking.

What dismayed me most about that next day (July 16) was the certain knowledge that we must carry the first loads up toward the base of the north face of Peak Nineteen. The thought of carrying 60 pounds of gear five to seven miles across moraines and black ice held virtually no appeal at all. One slight chance of escape from such labors remained in that two of our team's complement would have to remain behind. Marts was clearly excepted from carrying, as he was in charge of equipment for the entire American expedition. He had, therefore, to preside over the assignment of tents, ropes, hardware, and American rations to each of our teams. Additionally, another member of the team had to remain to organize our expedition gear and make the draw of Russian food supplies. Gary Ullin's emerging talent as a manager of detail made him a logical choice for this task. So, it was finally pretty obvious I would be better off going up with a load rather than hanging around Base in a somewhat disoriented condition.

It was also on that morning that the Soviets issued Russian-made transistor radios to the various teams. The radios were very small, almost toylike, and the thought of our sophisticated, dependable Motorolas languishing in Soviet customs continued to depress us.

As we lay on the grass in front of the tents, trying to get organized for the relay, we played tapes. The Beatles'

"Back in the U.S.S.R." seemed amusing at the time, but was grating. What Gary and I liked most was Cat Stevens's "I'm on My Way." Gary seemed to think that ought to be our expedition anthem. The song seemed to express many things for all of us, and I had no idea how prophetic it would prove to be.

The morning dragged on as we began to assemble the elements of loads. We would not have the requisitioned Russian food to carry until the next day—the Soviets felt they needed a day to decipher and fill out our lists—nor much of our prepackaged American freeze-dried high-altitude rations, as Marts was distributing the whole range of expeditionary supplies to the four teams. Roskelley and I assembled loads of 55 to 60 pounds, mostly tents, hardware, and cooking gear and, having delayed our departure in order to have some lunch, got away at around 2:00 P.M. I reasoned that a late departure promised a short march if we were to return to camp that night.

We set out from Base across the edelweiss-covered meadows, past flocks of sheep and the somewhat impassive but never unfriendly Kirghiz shepherds. We were at 11,700 feet, yet the length and apparent nutritiousness of the grass seemed hard to believe. Even though Kirghiz farms have been collectivized and are under the harsh Soviet bureaucracy, it is clear that these strong, elegant, uncomplicated people are still in harmony with their thriving upland meadows. These meadows were unlike any most of us had ever seen. Wild grasses and flowers extend in rolling waves into the midst of the major ice fields. There are absolutely no trees in this part of Kirghizia. The country is reminiscent of the Brooks Range and tundra slopes of northern Alaska in that respect. In the Karakoram, farther south, there are exquisite small meadows beside the glaciers, but much barren, unvegetated terrain; so too in the Hindu Kush. But in the Pamirs the old flat rolling moraines of the ancient glaciers seem to be paved with vegetation, and the grasslands roll up from the lower elevations for miles until they join the ice.

Our conditioning and the acclimatization on Rainier seemed to be paying off. Despite the hangover, I felt surprisingly strong; even to keep in sight of the phenomenal powerhouse Roskelley was an achievement in itself. Our objective was to find a simple, direct route through the complex crisscross of moraines at the confluence of the Lenin Glacier, which comes down off Krylenko Pass and Peak Lenin itself, and the North Face Glacier, issuing from the north face of Peak Nineteen. We passed from meadow to moraine rather abruptly, seeking to force a direct line to the key moraine on the far side of the glacial torrent pouring out of the Lenin. The going wasn't all bad, deteriorating only as we got to the active black ice of the main glacier, where mud, suspended gravel, and free-balanced boulders overlaying the polished ice threatened an ankle sprain or worse at every step. On the whole, Pamirs glacial moraines, and those of the Karakoram and Hindu Kush to the south, seem considerably less precarious and dangerous than those of Alaska and northern Canada.

Roskelley insisted on attempting a crossing of the roaring stream cascading down from the gravel-blackened snout of the Lenin Glacier. I tried to humor John with bets that he wouldn't get past the second braid in the stream (I was sure he couldn't pass the first), and the question "By the way, how in hell do we get out of the stream and up the almost vertical gravel bank on the opposite side?"

"Oh, it'll go, Big Daddy! I just know it will. I mean, I think I can make it. Don't you *really* think I can make it, Bob?"

"John, I'd like nothing better than to get rid of this goddamned load and hightail it back to Base, but if you go into that stream, even with a rope on you, I'm afraid you won't make it. You'd probably drown."

Roskelley paced the bank like a caged animal, trying to

find some weakness in the stream. There was none, only grinding boulders under the surface of the sullen, angry brown roaring water. Finally, it was as if John had completed a ritual within himself in which reason was first put aside and then reinstated; he turned away from the stream and said, "Okay, Dad, let's go up the snout and across to the sandbar on the other side."

We cached our loads on the east bank of the Lenin where one of the lateral moraines on the North Face Glacier abutted the main body of the Lenin. The way ahead to Peak Nineteen looked straightforward.

Our return to Base in the last evening light was gratifying. "Mash," as we had dubbed ourselves, was the first team into the field relaying loads, and there was a real sense of momentum. Gary and John were excited and cheered that we had found a relatively straightforward route toward the base of the north face. Marts, however, was still not feeling well.

We sat around the mess tent writing postcards and letters. We'd all be heading out for our objectives soon. No mail had come, and I recalled that on K2 in 1953 we had received letters three days after we reached Base Camp, and I remembered as well how important mail is to expedition morale. Two quite pretty women sat at the table usually occupied by the Russians, with two of the Masters of Sport, Oleg and Kostya. The older woman was a striking blonde, probably in her early thirties; the younger was brunette, with a round cheerful face and lovely complexion. They were very animated. We had heard there was a team of women, several of the best female climbers in the Soviet Union, training for the first all-women ascent of Peak Lenin. They were going to do a demanding traverse of the peak up from the east on the Lipkin ridge to the summit and down the Razdelny on the west. The blonde was really stunning. She seemed to be named "Elvira," but was usually addressed by such diminutives as "Viretska" and "Eliashna."

Michael Monastyrski had told me there were ten "girls," as he called them, and that they were like his daughters. He spoke of them with great pride and real paternal affection; there was no offer to introduce us to them, but one sensed their business was too serious for social contact. For the most part the women remained across the creek in the "Soviet Nationalities" camp. They made several practice climbs, and we observed them a couple of times doing calisthenics in front of their tents. We got the impression that these ladies ranging in age from 22 to 35 were very serious; the male Soviet climbers reinforced the impression of their seriousness, noting that several of the women had done very big climbs in the Caucasus and the Tien Shan and that one or two had been up Lenin via the Razdelny route in a mixed party of men and women. They were clearly well disciplined; still they sang songs together, and not infrequently we would hear their excited chattering and their laughter tinkling like bells across the valley.

Our strong Lenin–east face team, led by John Evans, began to get into gear. On July 17, Pete Lev, Fred Stanley, Jeff Lowe, and Al Steck started up for the Pass of the Travelers with loads, planning to establish a camp before the base of the grueling, dangerous climb to Krylenko Pass. Evans was still feeling ill and decided to rest one more day. Schoening's group of Marty Hoey, Chris Kopczynski, and Frank Sarnquist were champing at the bit; and Pete, despite his continuing misery from the kumiss, got them off with relays for their long journey to the unexplored, unclimbed peaks of the Dzerschinsky Glacier region.

Jock Glidden's team, whose objective was the formidable unclimbed east face of Peak 6852 (22,480 feet), was slow in getting up a head of steam. What was emerging was a conflict of personalities. Jock had cheerfully relinquished his preferred role as a member of the Evans powerhouse in order to lead the Peak 6852 team. What he seemed to be getting in his team were two strong, seasoned climbers, Jed Williamson, with more expeditionary experience than the rest, and Mike Yokell, a very competent technician on rock and mixed snow and ice. The fourth member, Molly Higgins, was our least experienced technical climber, especially in snow and ice glacier travel, but she did not lack enthusiasm, and despite her tendency to be overly cheerful before breakfast (in the eyes of some of the more crotchety climbers), her positive attitude proved a real asset. She acquitted herself very well throughout the summer. The fifth member of the team, Chris Wren, had climbed in Alaska and Europe and, though not as technically and physically strong as some of the other Americans, had the capacity to become a helpful, contributing team member. He definitely proved this later with Glidden and Steck on the Lipkin ridge of Peak Lenin.

Both Williamson and Yokell felt that the team's potential and the probability of success on 6852 were threatened by Molly Higgins's inclusion in the group. Their discontent began to be felt in the other groups. When it surfaced openly, I approached Jed and Mike and told them they were behaving like a couple of jerks and that they could stay behind if they weren't prepared to make their team work. I pointed out what was obvious to all of the rest of us—that they had the potential of two quite strong load carriers in Molly and Chris and that the real fun of pioneering the difficult climbing and route finding on 6852 would fall on the three others. Clearly, Jock Glidden bought this thesis, but somehow it didn't sit well with Jed and Mike. They wanted to be members of a uniformly strong powerhouse team; yet in Glidden and themselves, plus the two willing, less experienced climbers, they had more than enough potential to mount a first-rate effort. Glidden, a climber of real talent and compassion, understood the variables and the problem. Glidden noted with almost surgical detachment in his diary:

BASE CAMP UNDER THE "ROOF OF THE WORLD"

I. My surprise at being assigned leader of a group—not my expectations (which were to look after only myself, just do a hard route)—this causes me to revise my role, presents me with a social as well as physical challenge.

II. Why a social challenge: to wed the group among which were two dissidents, Mike Yokell an experienced climber, tagged on at the last minute as an alternate, and Jed Williamson an experienced outdoorsman (not as technically accomplished as Mike).

III. Their Complaints:
   A. Personnel were not as advertised:
      1. Molly Higgins—young, O.B. [Outward Bound] instructor, no expeditionary or snow and ice experience.
      2. Chris Wren—N.Y. Times correspondent, obviously appeared inexperienced.
   B. Above inexperience and incompetence would endanger their lives.
   C. Above inexperience and incompetence would prevent them from doing a hard route.

I felt these complaints justified, but they avoid the larger, more important points: (1) we must make the best of our situation and I felt we could do well anyway; (2) alternative was to quit; (3) U.S. team here to climb as cohesive units—not to appear divisive.

As it turned out, Jock's team shook down fairly quickly on the way up Krylenko. As the days passed, I felt bad about sounding off at Jed and Michael. I liked them both, and I knew Jock's team would do well with any kind of luck. My impatience and momentary anger with them were rooted in what I discerned to be a lack of confidence in themselves. I'm not sure this was ever understood.

CHAPTER FOUR
▲
Trouble on Krylenko

As "Mash" set out for Peak Nineteen, we sensed that we were undertaking one of the very best climbs of the summer. We were also aware of the extremely challenging objectives of the other teams. We felt our overall objective was perhaps the most ambitious of the summer: not only to climb the untried direct face of Peak Nineteen, but also to descend the west ridge, establish a cache in 19,095-foot Krylenko Pass (mostly equipment), descend to Base for ten days' more supplies, and return to attempt one of the east face routes on Lenin. How ambitious, if not naive, this itinerary was may be seen by considering the luck of those who went to the east face.

Jock Glidden's team had a far more formidable objective in the unclimbed east face of Peak 6852 (Moscow-Peking) than was realized by most of the Americans. In its main assault phase, the climb would entail at least 5,000 feet of steep ice climbing. There would be resting points, but the route would be intricate and the climbers would be constantly exposed to the danger of ice avalanche. In some segments the climb seemed (from the pictures we had seen) to be technically demanding. This had to be in Jed's and Mike's minds as they got upset over what they thought were weak links in the team.

Moreover, Peak 6852 was well beyond Peak Lenin and would require at least an additional day of relaying. Jock's group was also expected to traverse along the 6852-Lenin ridge from south to north, and to finish their route on top of Lenin, thence descending via the Razdelny col.

Pete Schoening's group, bound for the Dzerschinsky Glacier area west and southwest of Peak Lenin, had the least-defined goals of any of the American teams. What made their plans attractive was the promise of discovery. There were no photographs of any of the peaks, no information on the glacial terrain which had to be traversed; there was just one oblique aerial photo which could have been a segment from the Greenland ice cap, containing virtually no definition of the contours of the peaks.

The Soviet climbers who had looked into the Dzerschinsky Glacier affirmed that there were indeed some striking mountains and difficult routes, but there was nothing specific beyond that. They had not exaggerated, as indeed it appears there are vast untouched areas of the Pamirs which the Soviets are in no hurry to open up for climbing exploitation by either their own or foreign mountaineers. With so much emphasis on sports, and seemingly so much official encouragement of sports in the U.S.S.R., it seems a mystery that any peaks would remain unclimbed. On the other hand, they may be simply conserving an inventory of appealing objectives which, properly apportioned out, cannot eventually fail to attract foreigners and the favorable inflow of foreign currency which the Soviets seem very concerned to seek.

There are other anomalies too: Why had the north face of Peak Nineteen not been climbed when its upper 3,000 feet were virtually in sight of the long-established Base

Camp? The direct route on the face is no minor undertaking, yet there is no record of its having ever been tried. Conceivably some earlier attempt was made that ended in tragedy, but if so, like so many other histories in Russia, it lies locked below the surface of memory or record.

Pete's group clearly had the toughest logistical task: to relay some 25 days' supplies about twelve miles up to approximately 20,000 feet, then push on another eight to ten miles into a virtually unknown region. In some ways it was also most daring: to climb a number of untried peaks rising above 20,000 feet that were suspected to be of substantial difficulty. This was reminiscent of early Alaska climbing days or of the great pioneering explorations and ascents of Schneider and Aschenbrenner in the Cordillera Huayhuash in the Peru of the 1930s. It was quite possible that they would uncover the best climb of the summer.

The one climb that undoubtedly had an international classic character was the middle buttress of the east face of Peak Lenin. It was, we all agreed, as Jeff Lowe quietly remarked on looking at the Austrian photo which became our expedition postcard, "a real mother!"

The east face of Peak Lenin is a fairly broad 7,000-foot wall, marked by a series of distinct ice ridges that tumble steeply down from the summit plateau of the mountain. Between the ridges are ice-swept couloirs and avalanche-polished blue ice slopes. The ridges are largely buttressed by bulging ice cliffs, segments of which seem to slough off to the sides or to discharge directly onto the knife edges and bulges below. The average angle of the ridges in the center face appears to be above 50 degrees with numerous short pitches exceeding 70 degrees.

Two routes on the east face had been climbed before. The Austrian ridge in the southeast quadrant of the mountain, forming the left-hand margin of the east face, and lying back somewhat from the more consistently steep gradient of the main wall, has been climbed by several parties

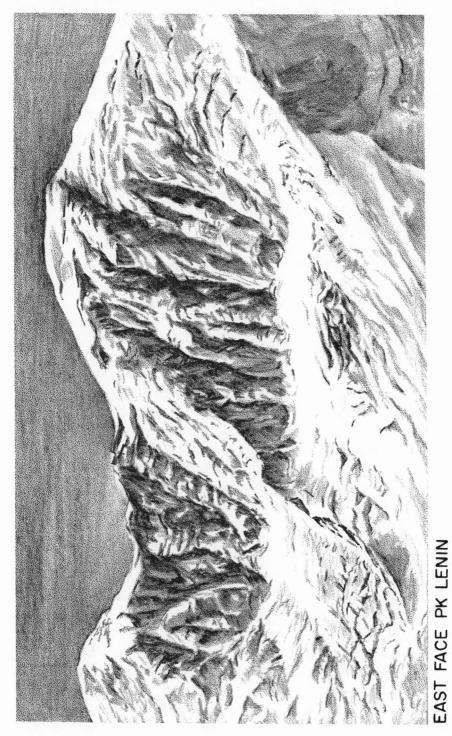

EAST FACE PK LENIN

Pk 6852 on left

and constitutes a respectable, though not unusually hard, climb. Some of the best mountaineering is found on the steep knife-edge ridge at the base.

The Hiebler ridge, named because of its first ascent in 1967 by a combined Russian-Austrian party led nominally (at least according to the Russians) by an Austrian, Tony Hiebler, is a different matter. The Hiebler route, which is the last distinct ridge on the right-hand side of the east face, starts abruptly from the last flat shelf of the Saukdhara Glacier, beginning with a steep avalanche-swept ice slope which leads from the left to a poorly defined ramp, then onto a hanging ice tongue which discharges frequently onto the glacier below. An alternate approach can be made from the right, but involves crossing a large, very active ice discharge gully of dubious reliability. The approach to any part of the east face, save the Austrian ridge, is exposed and potentially quite hazardous.

The Hiebler is a hard route, clearly a major grade VI climb, which, on the first ascent, required seven days. Hiebler reported four days of 70-degree ice climbing with no letup. The climb is made between 17,000 and 23,400 feet, with virtually no opportunity for exit off the route once one is committed, save rappeling down the route of ascent. In prolonged bad weather, the east face is a potential nightmare. In good weather, its routes offer some of the most difficult sustained climbing to be found anywhere.

The route Evans's team would try, the main center ice ridge, appeared to be steeper and somewhat longer than the Hiebler and to offer considerably more individual problems—especially a series of ice bulges conceivably approaching the vertical and extending up the ridge several thousand feet.

As the American plans for the east face developed and the climbers of Evans's group got under way with loads up the Lenin Glacier, others too were heading for the east side of Lenin. A very strong English team led by Doug

Scott and including Paul Nunn, Tut Braithwaite, Clive Rowland, Guy Lee, and Speedy Smith was out in front of the Americans and intent on doing a route on the east face, though it never became clear precisely what they had in mind. We presumed they would be trying something to the right or left of the route the Russians had agreed would be "reserved" for a first try by the Americans.

At the same time the teams were heading for Krylenko Pass, there was a mass of Austrians, some Swiss, two old Italians, and some of the Dutch moving out for the west side of Peak Lenin and Camp III on Razdelny Pass (19,685 feet). Pete Schoening's group threaded its way through this international traffic seeking entry to the Dzerschinsky Glacier. In addition to the Americans on the north face of Peak Nineteen there were two German teams and two ropes of French climbers, all of whom were doing a previously climbed route on the northwest ridge. A group of Dutch climbers sought peaks to the east of Nineteen, as did the ambitious Scots.

From the south and up the more direct route of the Saukdhara Glacier ten Estonian climbers were bound for the east face, intending to do the Hiebler route. We could never find out very much about that group, but envied their easier access to the face, circumventing the steep, tiring, and potentially dangerous avalanche slopes leading up from the Lenin Glacier onto Krylenko Pass. That route was available to them inasmuch as they were not a part of the International Camp. If the various international teams had opted for or been allowed to choose the Saukdhara, the administrative cohesiveness of Base Camp might have been jeopardized. The Soviets reasoned, as far as we could tell, that any foreign team (i.e., Western European, Japanese, or American) that could not be monitored (for reasons of safety) by Base Camp radio would create an undesirable and potentially embarrassing situation.

The Soviets, understandably, desired to control as much

as possible of the activity in the Peak Lenin region from the north side. They seemed to reason that their attempt at setting up an international meeting of climbers was far more important than the expeditionary desires of various national climbing teams. To the extent that reasonable climbing objectives could be undertaken and achieved from the Achik Tash Valley, they were fairly disposed to granting permission to the foreign climbers to make attempts. Underlying all of this, however, they were basically obsessed with getting as many foreign climbers to ascend Peak Lenin (by whatever route) as possible.

The Russians are as aware as anyone of the romance and challenge of new summits and new routes; but they are also ceremonialists as well as sports politicians, and the opportunity to focus an outstanding international congregation of mountaineers at the shrine of Soviet mountaineering was not missed. The symbolism of group achievement seems to have an almost mystical appeal for some Soviet mountaineers, and no doubt derives from Communist political and economic ideology.

This spirit was reflected in an interview in *Komsomolskaia Pravda* (October 21, 1973) with Vitaly Abalakov, the dean of Soviet mountaineering, who became our friend during the summer of 1974. When he was asked to identify the peculiarities characterizing the Russian school of mountain climbing, Abalakov replied, "First of all, fully developed collectivity and unitedness are evident. Obviously, alpinism is an extremely collective activity. An individual would be absolutely helpless in the mountains. The teamwork means more than competence for climbing with companions on one rope. It also does not only mean that one is ready to take risks in one's partner's name. The most valuable thing is the skill of falling into line with the goal of the whole party."

The collective attitude deeply ingrained in Soviet mountaineers came into sharp contrast from time to time with the European and American climbers' more characteristic attitude of individual responsibility in crisis situations.

John Evans's team of Carson, Lev, Lowe, Stanley, and Steck were off with heavy loads on the morning of July 17 bound for the Pass of the Travelers and the Lenin Glacier fork leading to the Krylenko headwall. Seldom in American mountaineering history has a stronger, more diversified, better balanced team of climbers been assembled.

It was a compatible team of distinct individualists. The glue seemed to be the two oldest climbers, Evans and Steck, but each man was contributing to a sense of cohesiveness, and all had the capacity to lead whenever the situation demanded. It had quickly become a happy, smooth-working team.

Jock Glidden's team had pulled itself together, working on group coordination, after a training climb on the ice peak above Base Camp, and a growing spirit of teamwork had developed by the time they reached the base of the Krylenko face.

Evans's party was a day ahead of Glidden on the Krylenko slope, and the English were a day ahead of John. The Japanese teams were moving supplies in between. The international traffic was heavy on Krylenko and friendly. National teams alternated trail breaking, and the Americans advised the less experienced Japanese on avalanche hazard.

The climbing on Krylenko was alternately hot and exhausting and cold and exhausting. The morning heated up steadily, then shortly after noon gave way to consolidating cumulus clouds and intermittent snow squalls which by midafternoon settled into a steady snowfall. The Krylenko slope is a broad glacial headwall that rises some 5,000 feet above its 15,000-foot base and provides some of the hardest, most tedious uphill carrying anywhere. There are no technical difficulties to speak of, a few large well-defined crevasses one must thread through on the moderately steep but monotonous slope, and the persistent nagging awareness that under avalanche conditions the Krylenko face would offer virtually no escape.

Evans's team carried rapidly up the Krylenko face, reaching Crevasse Camp with a second relay at 18,000 feet on July 21. The camp was so named because it was situated on the partially shoveled-out lower lip of a very large crevasse, with an overhanging upper lip that jutted out over the tents some 35 to 40 feet. Crevasse Camp seemed to be the only really safe place on the entire face. The English team led by Doug Scott had arrived the day before and put the track into the top of Krylenko Pass, and after a night's stay all six Americans moved up with full loads and across the Pass at 19,095 feet to a cache close under the east face of Peak Lenin.

As they crossed over onto the southeast side of Krylenko Pass, the group gained a whole new sense of the Pamirs Range. To the east and into China, some ten to twenty miles away, there were ranks of big ice-covered peaks beyond which one could make out the endless dry desert wastes of Sinkiang Province. To the south, the complicated and impressive east face of Peak 6852 glistened in the weak sunlight; and more directly in front of them as they descended, the huge ice wall of the east face of Peak Lenin rose from 17,000 to almost 23,500. The great Saukdhara Glacier flowed south and around to the west beyond Peak 6852, having its origin in the enormous ice cirque formed by Peak Lenin and the mountain that had been known as Moscow-Peking, then Unnamed Peak, and then simply 6852.

As they approached the ice hummock they had selected as a cache site, Carson, Lev, and Lowe were proceeding unroped, followed by Evans, Stanley, and Steck, who had elected to remain tied in. A good thing it was that they did, for Steck, following in the track made by the others, broke through a bridge and plunged out of sight twenty feet into a quite large hidden crevasse. Steck, the always laconic veteran, soon worked himself up and out of the crack, using jumars on the tight rope, commenting on the crevasse as he emerged, "When you've seen one you've seen them all."

As they cached gear and food at the base of the east face, the Americans—now joined by the English at the cache—spotted a team of five climbers working their way up the Hiebler ridge at about 19,000 feet. Presumably these were the Estonians we had heard rumors about, as Evans's group knew of no other team that had come up the Saukdhara, and certainly no one else had come over the Krylenko. At almost the same moment, they noted a camp with several tents closer under the east face and assumed these were other climbers in support of the teams on the Hiebler ridge. As the American and English climbers left the cache, the sun was beginning to be lost in the clouds, and mist was enveloping the ropes of two or three Estonian climbers on the Hiebler as they approached the first big ice bulge on the ridge. The route did not look at all easy. The central buttress looked a good deal worse.

As the group regained the crest of Krylenko Pass, it had been snowing quite hard, with little wind, and the temperature seemed very warm. The air was close and heavy even for that altitude. Peter Lev was very uneasy about the snow condition that had apparently developed in a very short time; and while he couldn't state precisely what was taking place, he sensed the slopes had become ominously avalanche-prone.

Pete dug a number of core samples and said finally that the snow seemed to be in a slab-avalanche condition. But they all knew that there had been virtually no wind action of any consequence during the period of change in snow structure. The climbers were extremely apprehensive and there was serious discussion about the wisdom of even descending to Crevasse Camp. They finally decided to go down with the hope of carrying all the remaining supplies to the east side the next day.

Doug Scott and his team decided to return to Base that afternoon, July 22, for more supplies, with a possible stopover at the foot of the Krylenko. Evans's group cooked dinner in a mood of great unease. They envied the English for their straightforward decision to return. The huge overloaded unstable snow mass above them could let go at any moment, sweeping everything off the face. Still, by staying high the Americans could gain a considerable jump on the others intent on the east face.

As they prepared supper, one of the two stoves they carried appeared to have a problem with its stem cleaner and wasn't burning efficiently at all. They discussed whether they should go down to repair the stove and also whether the team should split up. A major consideration was that Jeff Lowe's knee, which had been reinjured on Rainier, was improving, but definitely suffered from downhill pounding. He wanted to avoid at all costs any chance of further damage. They talked far into the evening, and Al Steck, having had a full day of heavy load carrying and crevasses, had an anxious time lying in his sleeping bag thinking the group might resolve to break camp in the middle of the night and descend.

During the morning of July 23, the discussion about descending continued. It had snowed more, and the air was beginning to warm up and develop that peculiar closeness so many of the campers noted in various parts of the Pamirs that summer. Lev became convinced that a slab condition had developed as a consequence of sun action and the extremely dry air, which was causing accelerated sublimation with consequent weakening of the bonding properties of the new snow layers. He was not convinced it was even safe to descend below Crevasse Camp.

At about that same time, a fairly large group of Japanese climbers arrived from below at the camp, totally oblivious to the sudden change in snow texture and the developing avalanche hazard. When it was explained to them, not without difficulty and confusion, they stored their loads in an unoccupied sector of the great crevasse and immediately headed back down the mountain. A few moments later, Molly Higgins appeared, going strong and with a big load, followed by the rest of Jock Glidden's team. They too were unaware of the hazardous state of affairs, but didn't seem inclined to surrender their newly won position on the mountain.

By now Evans, Stanley, Carson, and Steck had decided they would head for Base Camp. Pete Lev and Jeff Lowe would remain at Crevasse Camp and make another carry over Krylenko if conditions improved. The four had decided to go down partly because they didn't feel secure at Crevasse Camp and partly to repair or replace the stove part and pick up additional supplies. There was no really central reason. Yet, as John Evans noted, "Nothing about the decision was very clear. We didn't want to split up, yet four of us felt uneasy staying on. The air had become strange and heavy and finally we just headed down."

As Jock's team had decided to stay, they loafed a bit in the growing heat, then began to seek out tent platforms. There were questions, in light of the newly identified danger, about the safest locations. Evans's group had two Bauer tents on the upper lip of the crevasse. Yokell felt they were too exposed to sloughing slides and certainly to a major avalanche coming down over the upper lip. As Carson, Evans, Stanley, and Steck headed down in the increasing snowfall and gloom, a heated discussion of the tent matter developed between Jeff Lowe, Mike Yokell, and Jock. Mike actually wanted to move one of the already pitched tents into the partially filled crevasse, an effort that would entail substantial digging and leveling. Jeff, having already made his home in the camp, felt it was an unnecessary effort. Yokell continued to protest, and Jeff with a certain finality retorted, "Well goddamnit, Mike, I'm a fatalist!"

Pete Lev had been feverishly assessing the changing snow conditions that dramatically altered in just 24 hours. He wrote of that moment, "I was distressed. Something was wrong. All that I knew (or thought I knew) about avalanches seemed to contradict the possibility of immediate danger. But the atmosphere was absolutely heavy with impending disaster."

An unusual situation was developing. As we later pieced it together, it was a slab-avalanche condition that had perhaps never before been observed by a trained snow specialist. Normally in slab conditions, the sublimation* of water vapor in the snow layers moves from the warmer snow to the colder atmosphere. In the Pamirs in 1974, Lev noted, "the combination of very dry, cold, clear nights at high altitude followed closely by a calm, clear day with a very hot sun produced a 'reverse sublimation'; that is, the development of a sun action slab that had not heretofore been observed." All this inverse sublimation had occurred in eleven or twelve hours, hence Pete's distress. All that was required was a trigger.

As Yokell and Lowe debated, Lev was anxiously watching his altimeter-barometer, noting a steep rise in the altimeter of 50 feet, which means a corresponding drop in barometric pressure. Avalanches have been known to be triggered by a sudden drop in barometric pressure. Clouds enveloped the Crevasse Camp; it became noticeably warmer, then began to snow. It was about 1 P.M., July 23.

Glidden wrote:

> ... a few minutes before the avalanche I was aimlessly wandering around the tents above the crevasse half resolved to

---

* Sublimation is the process by which water is converted directly from solid to vapor. Within the snow cover, the flow of heat is a complex phenomenon. Within some environments, up to half of the heat flow in snow is estimated to be due to sublimation.

take a nap. I was drowsy and tired from the hike and unac-
customed altitude. Around that time I had also been about
20 feet down the slope, (where the brunt of the avalanche
hit) adjusting a melt tarp. Had I either taken a nap in my tent
(later buried by the avalanche) or been at the melt tarp, I
probably would have been killed. I had just put all three
snow shovels together by the corner of my tent when I felt
the ground settle with a "whomp." Not realizing it was an
earthquake, I reasoned it was the snow settling as it does in
the spring during ski tours. The noise aroused me from my
torpor and caused a mild rush of anxiety to come over me. I
apparently checked the nature of the partly filled crevasse
below me from the corner of my eye and subconsciously
resolved I would dive in it at a certain spot if an avalanche
really came over the top.

Soon after the settling noise, I heard a crack and someone
yelled, "avalanche!" I did not look up to see, but from reflex,
dove head first into the very spot of the crevasse I had only
a moment before checked out; it was as if I had done it from
drill many times before.

The avalanche roared over my head for certainly no longer
than a minute—I am sure less—but it seemed the longest
minute in the world. I regained my footing in the crevasse
and I remember panting—gasping for breath—as the snow
swirled every place: down my neck and in my boots, but I
was not buried above the ankles. I did not think directly of
death and imminent suffocation but rather, "So this is what
an avalanche is REALLY like!" (I had never been in one
before.) I also wondered during that long minute whether
there was enough snow in the avalanche to bury me, only a
wild-eyed feeling of disbelief of what was happening.

When it stopped, I frantically called to Jeff, who was now
buried to the waist about 20 yards away, [to ask] whether he
and the rest were all right. Standing near Jeff was Peter
whose face was the picture of worry and fear. When I
learned everyone was safe, my franticness dissolved into a
mixture of urgency to do something and a detached interest
in what one does in such occasions. Jed and Jeff said I appeared indignant that this should happen to me at all.

I remember that my first bit of reflection was to approach

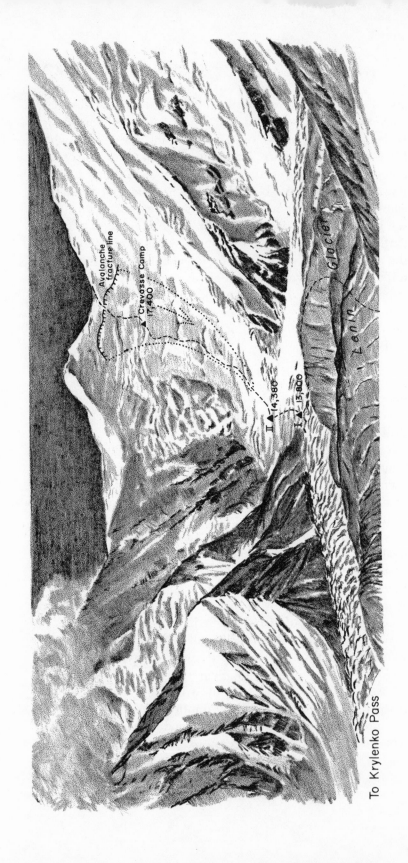

Avalanche fracture line

Crevasse Camp
17,400

II ▲ 14,386

I ▲ 15,800

Lenin Glacier

To Krylenko Pass

John Evans' team proceeding from Krylenko Pass down Saukdhara Glacier toward the East Face of Peak Lenin. The Chinese Pamirs are in the background.

The Peak Nineteen team at Camp II. From left, Gary Ullin, Bob Craig, John Roskelley, and John Marts.

Fred Stanley

John Evans

Allen Steck

A Kirghizian woman and child, and a camel, in the High Pamirs.

Frank Sarnquist

Bruce Carson

Molly Higgins, Pete Schoening, and Chris Kopczynski at the summit of Peak Lenin (23,406 ft.).

Peak Nineteen (left) and Krylenko Pass and Peak Lenin (right), where the Soviet women's team lost their lives.

Jeff Lowe on the slopes
leading to Krylenko Pass.

JOHN EVANS

Marty Hoey and Peter Lev.

Christopher Wren

Christopher Wren

Jed Williamson

ALLEN STECK

JOCK GLIDDEN

JED WILLIAMSON

ALLEN STECK

Mike Yokell

Jock Glidden

The site where six of the seven bodies of the Soviet women's team were found.

Gary Ullin's memorial stone (*left*) and the gathering of the International Group for the memorial service for all the dead climbers.

Jeff and admit to him with a nervous smile that we must live charmed lives. I reasoned so not because my Maker has kept me alive until the age of 39 in spite of my habit of courting danger, but that just plain luck [was] mixed with my ability to assess situations with sufficient accuracy to have a sense for "the last ditch exit." My landing just in the right spot of the crevasse seemed to confirm this feeling.

Later in the day a deeper, more sustained sense of fear did overcome me, while the fear experienced in the avalanche was sharp, superficial, and short-lived. As we descended the 4,000 foot face to Moraine camp, visibility deteriorated in the snow storm, yet I could hear avalanches rumbling from distant and not so distant unseen slopes. Much of the snow we descended upon had not avalanched and I was very worried that it too might suddenly go or some slope above which I could not see would slide on us. I felt terribly helpless on that immense snow slope below Krylenko Pass, hence my deeper fear.

Jeff Lowe was apparently as close as anyone in Crevasse Camp to having been killed in the avalanche. He wrote of the experience:

Yokell was insisting that we dig platforms in the slope of the crevasse and move our tents in. I thought the tents were okay where they were because it was obvious that most of any avalanche would pass right overhead; well I wasn't really certain of that, but it seemed so much trouble to dig large enough platforms in the steep slope inside the crevasse. "I'm a fatalist," I lied. "Go ahead and dig if you want, but I figure we're all right as we are."

Fifteen seconds later there was a noise like a limb being torn from an oak tree, and the ice dropped some and shook from side to side. Lev, who was nearest to me said, "Christ, what the hell was that!" More to reassure myself than out of real conviction, I answered, "Oh, just the ice settling." Then added, "I guess . . ." All the while I was moving toward the crevasse. I felt jumpy like a half-tame coyote in a crowd of

97

people. Not until later did we learn we had experienced an earthquake.

A few moments later it was no real surprise to hear the sound of the air being pushed along in front of the avalanche. When the snow came roaring over the lip of the crevasse, I had already made my leap and someone yelled, "Jump in the crevasse!"

The shock of landing inside the crevasse never came. Instead I was cushioned in mid-air by fine snow packing in around me from all directions. The slide seemed to go on for a long time and I thought I would be completely buried. I admitted to myself that I was probably going to die; it was likely that the others would be buried also. But I resisted the temptation to panic or give up. Swimming seemed to work for a moment, but by the time the worst of the avalanche had passed, the snow started to imprison me—beginning with the feet and quickly moving higher. I put my arms in front of my face and waited. I remember that the spurts of adrenaline my system was getting were almost painful.

The wait was short, however, and the pressure of snow pushing down on the back of my head and neck subsided quickly. When I looked up there was still enough dust in the air that everything was white, and vision was impossible. I remember yelling, "Pete, Pete, are you okay?" By the time he answered, the dust had settled enough so that I could see his misty silhouette. He was just eight or ten feet away. Soon after that I could see the others running about on the lip of the crevasse or climbing out of it and screaming things like, "Is anybody buried? Is everyone okay?"

Shortly it was ascertained that everyone was indeed okay, and I was the only person needing help. While Jed was digging me out, I thought of the people on the slope below. "Fuck, fuck, fuck," I thought. "They didn't have a chance; they're all dead."

Pete Lev has described the events from a different perspective:

I don't remember if it was the sound that warned us, but it must have been, because the upper overhanging lip of the big crevasse some 40 feet overhead blocked our vision of the awful slope directly above. Most of us had never heard an avalanche so close before, and I certainly hadn't heard one from this position. But we all knew instantly that the avalanche was coming. We had maybe 15 seconds. I was eight feet from the crevasse; I ran and jumped in. Jeff was near me, doing the same. The drop into the crevasse was about ten feet into the soft snow, and as I landed, I looked up to the high upper lip and saw, distinctly, a solid wall of snow shooting out, going incredibly fast, blocking out the sky in darkness and roar. Cold snow came in on me, burying me in the hole as I tried desperately to claw my way back out with bare hands, utterly without success. It went seemingly on and on. Perhaps a full minute, then stopped.

Fine grain snow is settling now, and it is snowing as well. I am buried to my knees. Jeff's calling from a few feet away asking if I'm still there. Yes. Jeff is buried up to his waist; I dig frantically. Jeff and I don't know yet . . . we may be the only ones left alive. What despair.

Molly Higgins may have been doubted as a viable team member at the outset, but by the time her group had reached Crevasse Camp, there was no question that Molly would do just fine. She had the following account of the earthquake and avalanche:

During the half hour after Evans' party departed down the slope and before the avalanche, I began a total inventory of my party's food. It was a pleasant half hour, warm with partial sun, the sorting and logging of food being fairly interesting busy work. It was good to be busy with something because the avalanche condition that existed and the beginning of snowfall were worrisome (there's a contradiction here; I remember both warm and partial sunshine, plus the beginning of snow fall).

Mike Yokell kept badgering everybody (especially Jock Glidden) that our camp was unsafe, that we must dig a snow cave in the serac. Glidden was pretty easy-going about the whole thing, said that we'd move the tents farther into the crevasse if it continued to snow. Glidden was considering crawling into the tent to eat lunch, read and nap.

I was unhappy about the decision to stay at Crevasse Camp when Evans' party retreated. I felt that if the danger was bad enough for Evans to retreat, we ought to do the same. I supported Yokell's effort to move camp farther under the serac. I thought a cave was an excellent idea. But I was pretty lazy at the time and was happy enough to let things be for the time being. I considered myself strictly a follower, my lack of experience relegating me to a position of doing what the folks who knew better decided.

About 15 seconds before the avalanche there was a creaking, groaning sound in the crevasse, unlike anything I'd ever heard. I left my food-sort area and joined the rest of the folks by the tents. "What in the name of heaven was that?" was generally being mumbled about.

The roar of the avalanche and the pouring down of snow occurred simultaneously. I immediately knew without the process of thinking, "This is an avalanche. I will probably be buried suddenly. It will be a sudden packing of snow upon me, sudden and complete claustrophobia and suffocation. This may be it, this may be the chop."

I stooped down against the wind and covered my face, remembering everything I'd ever learned about avalanches. The roar of the avalanche lasted a long time; I knew that it might be safer in the crevasse, but I was doing fine where I was and was unwilling to go moving about, maybe getting into a worse position for all I knew. The snowfall from the avalanche back-spin was so thick that I could not see. After 30 or 45 seconds, I was only buried to my ankles and realized that I might make it. I noticed Chris Wren by my side, I think he might have been there the whole time. I told him to cover his face, which he did. We were crouched down, side by side. The avalanche lessened and stopped.

I was amazed that I was alive. More amazed that upon looking about, everyone else was alive and fine, too.

I knew we ought to do something very quickly, but I couldn't figure out what it was, so I just ran about in little circles for 10 or 15 minutes while Lowe was being dug out (I had no idea he was buried until much later. I couldn't figure out why no one was out of the crevasse doing anything). I was not paying attention to anything. I think I was shocked, felt very hyperactive, but uncertain of how to direct my hyperactivity.

Glidden was in the crevasse untouched. Wren and Lev were wandering about stunned. Yokell began shouting instructions which nobody obeyed. When Lev and Lowe emerged from the crevasse, it was decided that we must dig out our equipment in order to survive the night. Three ideas were bandied about—stay until morning, stay until night, leave immediately. Yokell, Williamson and Lowe became the leaders. We began to dig, jumping into the crevasse when we heard avalanches (which were somewhere else in the area). Lev and I assumed watch for other avalanches; eventually I took charge of the food-making, a hot drink, and sorting out food to take with us.

After two hours of digging and the recovery of most of our gear, it suddenly became obvious that we must get off Krylenko soon. Powder snow accumulating on the bare glacier ice above would be an easy surface to slide on. We quickly packed enough food and gear to spend the night, and headed down the slope.

I experienced the greatest fear during that trip down Krylenko. The going was slow, the powder snow crotch deep, my load was heavy, and I was really scared that another avalanche would hit us. At the bottom of Krylenko my party thought Evans' group was dead. Steck and John Evans had been especially good friends to me; the thought of those two dead in all of that ugly debris hit close to my heart. "What in hell can all this be worth when nice guys like John, Allen, Fred and Bruce get the chop. These mountains are a bunch of fickle SOBs and I don't want anything to do with them if they're going to kill my friends."

101

Of the seven Americans at Crevasse Camp, only Mike Yokell had sustained any injury, having badly damaged his knee jumping for safety into the crevasse.

John Evans and his three companions left approximately a half hour before the earthquake triggered the huge avalanche that swept Crevasse Camp and the Krylenko face. To clear the slope they had to descend approximately 3,000 vertical feet. Going down, they were tremendously apprehensive; the snow could let go at any moment. Peter Lev had convinced everyone that Krylenko had become an avalanche time bomb.

The snow was so deep and soft that glissading to make time was out of the question. Al, Fred, Bruce, and John had to get down fast . . . they could feel it. Stanley had the answer: they would all put on their nylon wind suits and utilize the slick surfaces to hasten their descent, sliding mostly on their bottoms and backs. They made remarkable time. The clouds and mists had enveloped the face. It snowed and they felt the ominous heat.

They had reached a point where the main slope began to level out. Out of the dense mist came the roar of the enormous avalanche. John Evans, in the lead of his descending band, recounts their experience:

> The first thing I remember clearly was seeing Fred spin around and shout, "Avalanche." I remember the moving snow was full of blacks and brownish-white instead of pure white.
>
> We were both dashing to the right when we looked up and saw another avalanche coming at us from that side. I remember Fred shouting, "There's another one," and my first reaction was to cut back to the left. I had taken a step or two in that direction before I realized the futility of that course. I realized I was going to be hit and tried to ditch my pack and protect myself; I got my shoulder straps off but not my waist band when I figured I was out of time and hit the deck. I'm

not sure, but I think I lay in that position for a second or two before it hit me.

Perhaps "hit" is the wrong word, as it was very gentle. I was aware of being pushed down the slope but I was not tumbled or submerged; I doubt that I was carried more than 20 feet. I remember feeling I had stopped but I could still hear the roar and feel the ice dust settling and I was afraid to look up for a second or two. When I did, I saw that I had been pushed to the side and as I undid my waist band and stood up I shouted, "Is everybody okay?" I heard Fred shout from a hundred feet below that he was all right and I saw Bruce come to a stop at about my level but 50 feet to the left. He was unhurt but his legs were buried so I ran over and helped him out. Just about then I heard Fred cry, "Where is Allen?" I think the great river of snow was still thundering on.

Bruce and I scrambled over the great ridges of snow blocks calling alternately "Allen" and "Help." Fred was doing the same a hundred feet or so below us. He started working his way down and I went up, hoping to either get a response from our friends at the camp or to find some trace of the camp in the debris. We couldn't see the top, bottom or the other side of the slide because of the fog.

This went on for a few very black minutes, until Fred shouted from below that he'd found Allen. Bruce and I charged down the slope, ignoring Fred's admonition to bring the packs. When I got to Allen, Fred had already dug away the snow from around his face, which was bleeding a bit from a small cut. Allen was groaning and looked pretty bad; I ran up, put my hat on him, and loosened his pack which was keeping a lot of pressure on his torso. He was buried except for his head and upper back; as we dug him out it seemed every limb we came to was twisted at a strange angle. Two or three Japanese arrived about then, saying their doctor was coming, they also said their camp had been demolished but that all their personnel were okay.

Bruce Carson, also descending as rapidly as possible with Fred Stanley, Al Steck, and John Evans, at the moment of the avalanche would have agreed with the view from above. He wrote:

I heard a roar, and looked up. An enormous mass of snow was coming down, heading just right of us, so I started left. Then I saw another mass coming to the left, and I knew that I was dead. The whole slope was avalanching, and it didn't seem feasible that any of us would live. I just accepted the fact of my imminent death.

In spite of this, I kept running, first left a few steps, then back right after seeing the avalanche farther leftward, and then left again as I finally got things sorted out in my head. The old avalanche path was to the right, and that is what was to be avoided most. I think I took 20 or 30 steps left, until I saw the avalanche almost on me, and then I threw myself on the ground, head ducked, arms over head, and gasping for breath. I felt a wind and blowing powder snow, and thought that maybe we would survive after all, if it was all powder.

Then the main mass hit me. I was prepared to be thrown, hurled down the slope, but it just pushed me, and at that instant I knew I would live after all. I rode for perhaps 50 or 100 feet down the slope, getting a gentle massage by snow chunks as I went. It was really kind of fun. Though that thought just crossed my mind, I didn't dwell on it.

When the avalanche I was in stopped, my legs were buried, though not deeply. John, Fred and I were all yelling, trying to find who was safe. We could see the center portion of the avalanche still moving, with enormous blocks of snow rolling end over end.

John helped dig me out (he and Fred had been farther left) and we started yelling for Al, and searching. Fred headed downhill, while John and I looked level with us, and started working downward.

In the same way I *knew* that I was dead when I comprehended the size of the avalanche, now I *knew* that Al was dead. He had been closer to the old avalanche path, and must be buried. Looking across acres of snow that had just ground to a halt, it didn't seem like there was any hope.

104

Meanwhile, we were looking anyway. Fred found Al, a couple hundred feet lower, and we all rushed down. Maybe we were all going to survive it after all.

Al was buried up to his neck, with his left hand sticking out, and blood on the snow around him, and on his face. My first reaction was that his lungs were punctured by his ribs in the fall. We started to dig him out, not knowing how seriously he was hurt, but fearing the worst. He was moaning, and we dug as fast as we could without hurting him more.

My next big scare was when we got snow off his back. It was curving backwards, and he started moaning. "Oh, my back! Get the snow off my back!" There was no snow on his back, and I was wondering what we could do with a spinal fracture, with no litter and little manpower. I received another shock when we started to dig out his legs. They were so twisted and out of place it just didn't seem feasible that they weren't broken. However, when we felt them, they didn't seem broken, and Al didn't complain.

It was snowing and we were understandably freaked about being in the middle of an avalanche path, and so we did something perhaps we shouldn't have done: John lifted Al up from behind, and put him in a sitting position. If his back had been broken, this could have severed his spinal cord. I don't know if the others had thought of this, but perhaps they thought like me: there isn't too much chance of it, and if it was broken, it would be too much of a job to get him down to contemplate. The three of us certainly couldn't do it, so we would have to leave him there in the middle of the path, and put the tent up around him. If another avalanche didn't get him, we might be able to get back up with some kind of stretcher, but it was too much to contemplate, so John lifted, and Fred and I watched.

After Al had sat there for a couple of minutes, it was clear that he was bruised and battered, but there was nothing too seriously wrong with him, and our thoughts turned to those in the camp above. I yelled up a few times, but got no response. I asked John to yell next, because I figured his voice might match his size. He yelled, but still we heard nothing from above. The certainty of death I had felt for myself, and then Al, was now being transferred to the people up above, seven friends I thought I'd never see again.

A few hours later, Pete, Jeff, Jock, Molly, Chris, Jed, and Mike descended from Crevasse Camp, expecting at any moment to be swept away, somehow certain their four friends below could not have survived the enormous avalanche of 5,000 vertical feet triggered by the earthquake. As they reached the tongue of the great avalanche Lev continues his account:

Oh, the debris, acres and acres of debris: large heavy, damp-looking boulder-shaped heaps of snow. They could never have survived this. There is no way.

We reach the base of the face where we had left a cache on the ascent. Jed, on the lookout, insists that the cache is gone, but his words fall on deaf ears. Jed says that they, John, Allen, Fred and Bruce, must have picked it up on their way down. No reaction.

Krylenko moraine camp. THERE THEY ARE!!! Relief upon relief. Yes, the avalanche hit them. But they were almost to the bottom of the big slope, in a low angle area, on the edge of the final runout of the avalanche.

It was so close, so very close. Just within inches, nearly 11 of us came that close to being killed. I flashed back to the scene at Crevasse Camp just seconds after dust had settled, when I was thinking real hard, just like a little kid. "Oh, please, if we are all safe I promise to do this, and this, and this . . ."

The Americans returned to Base a very sober, shaken, and relieved assortment of climbers. Yokell had great pain and real difficulty in making the return trip. Al Steck had two ribs cracked and found it difficult to breathe. Jeff Lowe's knee had become inflamed again in the descent.

But they were all alive, and they had come incredibly close to death.

In the face of the earthquake and dangerous snow conditions, Monastyrski and Abalakov had sent radio messages urging all climbing teams back to Base. Some, it turned out, did not receive those broadcasts. The returning Americans wondered about Pete Schoening's group and "Mash." There was no other indication of trouble, save the reports by other national teams of the earthquake. Those who happened to be standing still or lying in their tents and felt the shock were the most impressed.

By the afternoon, it was obvious that a major storm had enveloped the Pamirs. The Americans continued to wonder what had happened to all the Colorado summer weather they had been promised. Only the first day, the day of our arrival, had the Pamirs been completely clear. By 6:00 P.M. on July 24, there were over five inches of snow on the ground at Base.

The Scots were back, and so were the Swiss, French, and English. Schoening was still out, as were some of the Austrians (Axt and part of his group) and the Americans on the north face of Peak Nineteen.

It snowed and stormed all night, and by the morning of July 25 there were ten inches of surprisingly dry new snow compressing the rows of Base Camp resident tents. At 8:00 A.M. around the communications tent there was suddenly much excitement. The radio operator, Valerian, shouted across the mall, and soon Abalakov and Gippenreiter were at the transmitter-receiver. The Mayday voice signal from one of the teams had come in followed by an SOS made by cutting in and out with the transmitting button. It was the American team calling from Peak Nineteen.

CHAPTER FIVE

▲

The North Face of Peak Nineteen

"Mash" had been gaining momentum toward Peak Nineteen by July 17, as Gary, John and I started out for our moraine cache with an even heavier second relay. Marts was still not feeling well, nor were a number of others, so we pushed off, planning our last relay for the next day. We could establish Camp I a short way from the north face of Peak Nineteen the following afternoon. It had clouded over and rained or snowed the past three afternoons, but that didn't hamper our efforts, and it was cooler traveling on the lower levels. New snow was collecting higher up, and we heard an occasional avalanche roaring down the main north face around the corner.

Gary got his first taste of an Asian glacier, crossing the muddy black-iced snout of the main Lenin Glacier, which was not unlike many glaciers of Canada and Alaska, only perhaps dirtier. Although the glaciers of the Pamirs receive much snow, they are said to be steadily losing their main mass to surface evaporation and frontal retreat.

Gary was excited and eager to get on the mountain. We

all were, but he was perhaps the most emotionally keyed up to do a really good climb of any of our team. Roskelley, always the impatient driver, unrelenting in energy, was not as demonstrably charged as Ullin, but between these two our effort was fired with real momentum from the very beginning.

The trip was uneventful save for a team of what appeared to be Russian military climbers (we had noted their camp enroute from Base) evacuating a sick man off the Lenin Glacier. The casualty was a young man who had the outward symptoms of high-altitude pulmonary edema. Apart from numerous comrades who carried him four to six at a time, he was attended by an affable, clean-cut-looking young physician who announced apropos of nothing that he was an anesthesiologist.

The Soviet military climbers appeared to be a mixture of Caucasian and Asian men. When they had carried their evacuee to the base of the long steep riverbank leading to the military mountaineering camp lying at the upper edge of the great edelweiss meadow some two and a half miles from Base, they commenced a most amazing long-line vertical haul from the river bottom to the meadow bench above. Fully thirty to forty men pitched in at various points to propel the sick man and his stretcher up a static line that appeared to be supported by the winch haul on a truck perched at the edge of the bank.

Returning to Base Camp the evening of July 17, we were still concerned with Marts's lingering flu. We resolved, come hell or high water, to be off for Peak Nineteen with the last relay from Base early the next morning.

As we left Base the morning of July 18, clouds were building on the high shoulders of Peak Lenin. Climbers of many countries were headed for a great variety of objectives. There was a sense of secrecy and of excitement. The International Camp was becoming quiet. Most of the 170 persons had left that day, with by far the largest number

109

bound for the Pass of the Travelers, which seemed to be the gateway to Peak Lenin.

We reached the cache by midday, adding 20 pounds to our 60-pound loads—leaving one more full relay—and pushed on up the lateral moraines of the Lenin and North Face glaciers, eastward toward the north face of Peak Nineteen. As we proceeded up the huge stagnant moraines, now encountering occasional herds of wild yak with their fierce-looking long-horned bulls, we noted another climbing team relaying loads toward Nineteen. We were quite sure they were French by the distinctive color of their parkas, and we began to wonder whether the Russians had kept their promise that the first attempt on the north face was to be American. Almost as we observed the Frenchmen, seemingly threading their way through the yak herds, we spotted two teams of two and three climbers fairly high on the northwest shoulder of Peak Nineteen on the Abalakov route. We believed these were Bavarians, from what they had said at Base about their plans, but we couldn't help wondering whether there was something we didn't know, some surprise awaiting us on "our" route on the north face.

Camp I we called "Meadow Camp," and it was one of the most beautifully situated any of us had ever made. At about 12,000 feet we found a grassy flower-covered meadow at the bottom of a steep morainal gully leading up to the main North Face Glacier. To our right and the south, the jumble of old grass-covered moraines led up to one of the northwesterly spurs of Peak Nineteen. A clear stream emerged from the face of the flower-covered moraine. The flowers were remarkable. Edelweiss grew like dandelions everywhere in the Pamirs; but those velvety white blooms seem to compete always with a wide variety of colorful high-altitude plants such as what appeared to be Kirghiz varieties of shooting stars, penstemon, gentians, and asters.

A herd of wild yak, the high-altitude distant cousin of

110

the bison, grazed on the more level grass-covered parts of the moraine. Occasionally they would shyly peek over the edge down at our camp. It seemed incongruous, for the huge bulls with their long sharp horns appeared very fierce and clearly in control of the landscape, until one reflected that man has been pursuing the yak for countless centuries as a source of food and for domestication as beasts of burden.

We pitched the Bauer Himalayan tent for the first time on the carpet of flowers, with the entrance toward the north face. To the north and farther around to the north and west, the Guardian Peaks became the horizon, and clouds building in the northwest around to the buttresses of Lenin completed our sky.

Shortly after the tent was pitched, amid substantial thunder and far-off lightning, our first downpour began. The clouds seemed to condense from distant billowing clumps of huge high cumulonimbus very rapidly into a consolidated stratal mass. It was not just a brief shower but lasted four to five hours. Gary had a simple, sound idea—make a rain fly of the melt tarp we were carrying for use higher up. We had been informed by the Soviets that there was never any significant rainfall in the Pamirs in the summer, so we had not provided for what unquestionably became one of the most unusual seasons ever recorded in Kirghizia. Gary's improvised rain fly saved us from much discomfort and time wasted drying out gear, for it rained or snowed every one of the next four afternoons. After that came blizzards.

From Camp I early the next morning, July 9, we made a relay back from the snout of the Lenin Glacier. We moved very quickly across the vegetated moraines to bring up the last of our supplies from the sandbar cache. The scenery was enjoyable in spite of sprinting in the wake of the likes of John Roskelley and Gary Ullin. I wondered if we might be lucky and spot a snow leopard; surely they must be around, waiting for a young yak calf to stray a bit too far.

The momentum carried us back through Camp I, where we made up the first relay loads for Camp II at the base of the north face and at the head of the North Face Glacier. Marts was still not well and remained in camp. Gary, John, and I made good time and began to realize the dimensions of the north face as we moved farther up the strangely inert, almost inactive surface of the high Asian glacier. Few fresh opening crevasses, no seracs, graveled surface, but somehow scrubbed granular ice. The glacier, in its main bed, appeared to be dying. The real kinetic energy was poised above in cliffs of ice that appeared static, almost dormant; but the appearance was belied by periodic discharges of cascading mass that pulverized on the flat surface below.

The ice fell fairly uniformly from the cliffs across the lower face, but two somewhat protected lines presented themselves directly through the middle. One offered an immediate problem: once beyond the first 200 feet of almost vertical ice, the route through the center of the ice wall seemed fairly direct and reasonably safe. Unfortunately, the first 200 to 500 feet of the steep ice tongue seemed to be collapsing onto the floor of the main glacier. It might hold together as we made one pass, but it was not a route on which to relay loads.

Still, it was truly elegant. Roskelley didn't think it was worth trying; Gary thought it would go. I agreed with John that a hard but safer line lay to the left. Getting on and into a direct route on the north face seemed to be the most immediate problem, and some of the hardest climbing on the face appeared to be on the lower third. The final 3,000 feet seemed steep and demanding as well. There were plenty of uncertainties on the face as a whole, so we turned to what appeared to be an entry that would at least get us well into the climb with only a modest degree of initial danger.

What became our route on the north face was really a series of steep water ice steps that led up just to the left of the face's center, starting rapidly at about 48 to 55 degrees, linked by a tricky, dangerous exposed avalanche gully in which we came to achieve some fairly light-footed high-altitude sprints. The ice steps were fairly long and sustained high-angle pitches up to 70 degrees, over which heavy loads would have to be relayed. These constituted about 2,000 vertical feet of continuous steep climbing. Above that the slope gave way to steep—45 to 55 degrees —crevassed, and hanging glacier terrain for another 1,180 to 2,000 feet, which yielded a series of benches on which camps could be placed up to about the 17,300–foot level. We would put in two more camps, one at about 16,000 and another at 17,500. The final 3,000-foot water ice slope with its fish-shaped rock island presented itself as the last obstacle to the summit. All in all, a clean, classic, and very elegant direct route.

On July 19, we made a cache for Camp II on a morainal rib standing back off from the north face of Nineteen and, we hoped, beyond range and blast of the ice avalanches that came down at all times of day and night. We were not fully convinced that we might not get our tents blown down, but we were pretty sure we wouldn't be engulfed by avalanche debris.

Another and final relay from Camp I on July 20 after another afternoon of rain squalls and new snow above, and we established Camp II at the base of the north face. Marts had also carried up and, though still not in his best form, seemed better. John, Gary, and I decided to relay loads partway up the first section of the ice wall after we had pitched the Bauer.

The ice slope started modestly enough with an almost ideal tough granular texture for crampons, and then accelerated in steepness in a series of pitches. We knew from our perspective at Camp II it would be much steeper and more sustained above. We frontpointed a 50-degree bulge, traversed a short 70-degree buttress (which Roskelley did unroped), and ended on a small platform formed by the collapse of an old serac into a crevasse. Our cache was about 500 or 600 feet above camp, and the steepness and hard texture of even this first section of ice made us very respectful of what lay ahead. Our loads hadn't been heavy, perhaps 40 pounds, but we knew from the trend of the slope and the ice avalanche gully we had to cross above that the next section of the climb would require all our skill and determination, not to mention reasonable weather. As we descended, the sky had taken on its by now characteristic sheetlike cirrostratus quality, and it was raining fairly hard by the time we reached the tent and John Marts. John, who carried heavy to Camp II, while feeling poorly, had prepared hot tea and soup for our return.

We had the first of a series of great dinners that night (July 20) in which we utilized our varied and mixed diet of Russian and American (freeze-dried) food. The first course was red caviar on thin slices of Russian bread. Slices of Dutch cheese and Russian sardines (which they called "sproats") followed. The main course was freeze-dried beefsteak with broccoli and cheese. For dessert we had a tasty chocolate pudding and took in large amounts of tea to compensate for the increasing high-altitude problem of dehydration.

Conversation was animated with the excitement of breaking through the first big problem confronting us for the morning. The little we had done made us know it would be a sustained and fairly technical climb. We didn't like the discharge gully we had to go up and across; but we knew it would be brief. As it grew dark and the rain let up, the overcast sky became suffused with a faint saffron tint that seemed designed to go with the distant browns and greens of the Achik Tash. It was a peaceful place until the first of a series of ice avalanches of that evening roared down the face.

The morning of July 2 we were up and off early. The ice discharge gully above the cache was much in our minds, and we knew we had a day's work on the ice slope beyond. Marts was still sick; he wanted to carry loads and was discouraged that he could not. We felt another day's rest for him could be crucial later.

We put together loads that, combined with supplies at the cache, would go around 65 pounds, heavy for a couple of thousand feet of ice and steep glacier climbing. We moved up to the cache in almost half the time required the previous afternoon. Even as we got there, a small but ominous discharge of stones and ice came down the gully.

When we had reloaded the better portion of the cache into our packs, we poised on the edge of the gully like three sprinters. Gary and John, two of the fastest movers with whom I have ever shared space on a mountain, allowed me to start first and then passed me in a burst of speed that had us all chuckling, even as we anxiously eyed the ice wall at the head of the gully. We made the safe upper-right-hand side out of breath and in time to observe a freight train of downward-bound rock and ice.

The traverse up and right was menacingly steep and exposed. Roskelley led our team of three, who were now roped, cutting handholds, frontpointing in traverse, working toward a bulge on which we could turn and move directly, if not straight up. When we turned on the almost vertical bulge, which was in effect a slight ridge descending from the main and continuous ice face of about 400 feet above, we found a slight respite of 45- to 50-degree ice which gave us a breather to consider what lay ahead. The slope accelerated in steepness above in glistening granular ice, culminating in what appeared to be a slightly overhanging bulge. Beyond that, we recalled, the slope lay back some, then gave way to a series of steep ice and snow steps up and through which we had to thread our way over and around a series of overhanging crevasses and seracs.

Roskelley belayed Gary up to a platform he had cut at the beginning of the new steepness which curved up from

50 degrees. He had placed two pins, one ice screw for anchor and a warthog for security, and then Gary brought me up on the rope to his belay stance. I tied off a loop to the anchor as John moved out again.

Good ice climbers on demanding leads, moving with grace and rhythm though heavily laden, encumbered by gear and exposure, are not unlike the best powder-snow skiers; pushing the limits of snow and slope in a sort of high-angle dance form, they seem to stop time in the transformation of steepness into a kind of sculpture that vanishes even as it is created. Roskelley had that sort of grace, as did Gary, and that day was one of hard, exhilarating movement up the north face of Peak Nineteen.

Roskelley placed eight more pins as the route moved up directly and then angled left and over the final short bulging ice wall. The pitches had gone to over 70 degrees with the final bulge near vertical. With heavy loads this was both tiring and nerveracking. The exposure below down to the ice rubble was like that of a big rock wall. After the final bulge, the slope lay back to 50 degrees, then 40, and finally ended in a sloping benchlike platform on which the three of us stamped out a small lunch table. Clearly, the crux of the lower half of the north face had been solved by John's inspired effort. We felt a tremendous sense of relief to be off the ice wall, but we knew there was still a great deal of hard climbing ahead.

After sproats, crackers, cheese, and lemonade, we pushed up and to the right, centering ourselves close to the middle of the upper north face. We moved through short steep pitches of water ice covered by varying amounts of new snow, crossing over or detouring around a network of crevasses and seracs on sections of hanging glacier varying from 35 to 50 degrees. Extremely tiring going. To our exertions was added intense stifling heat as the sun beamed through a thin cloud layer onto the windless heat-reflecting glacier.

The climbing was demanding; the slope was deceptively steep and required belays from time to time. We frontpoint traversed several steeper sections, climbing simultaneously as much as possible. We were getting well up onto the face; Camp II was all but lost in the avalanche debris at the base of the wall. Around 3:00 P.M., after a long traverse right threading through a series of avalanche-filled crevasses and up onto a projecting hummock, we decided we had reached what would be Camp III. We checked the altimeter: 15,400 feet. Just about 4,000 feet to go!

We wondered what was happening to the others. Whatever happened to that Bavarian girl Anya? Anya was not only a capable mountaineer but an occasional model as well, and we had kidded Gary that she had a crush on him. Perhaps she was in that group we could now see high on the northwest shoulder. They appeared to be a day's climb from the summit. The thought that the Bavarians and French were on Peak Nineteen was not troublesome, for they were doing an established route and no one had ever, as far as we could find out, been on our route. The upper north face soared overhead, and we saw the climb in a new dimension, the last 3,000 feet rising in an unbroken slope of 60- to 70-degree blue ice.

We cached our loads in a gully leading up to the camp platform, then started down, remaining roped but moving continuously, save for a couple of the most delicate traverses. The unconsolidated snow balled up in our crampons, and it was clearly no place for a slip, as we were directly over the almost vertical section of the north face ice wall. Below, occasional avalanches roared out from the base. Descending a moderately steep section of snow over ice, I lost my footing and had to roll into an ice axe arrest position. Before stopping, I pulled Roskelley off balance, and he too had to make an arrest. There was nothing below but space. A reminder. We continued down with added caution.

We were elated as we descended from the Camp III

cache. We now had the key, and although what remained was hard work and some steep, demanding climbing above our final Camp IV, it looked as though we could definitely punch a direct route through to the top of the face. Weather was still a question. But we had heard the rather vague history of Pamirs weather suggesting it was not much different from summer weather in the Colorado Rockies, so we felt reasonably confident at that time. If there was any uneasiness or suspicion about our situation, it was that things were going too well in our strange and hostile environment. The fact of being in Soviet Asia and climbing hard routes in that remote and exotic area of the world gave an even greater sense of unreality to our situation.

We reached the top of the ice slope and our luncheon ledge at about 4:00 P.M. The hardest part of a long hard day fell away at our feet. The experience of climbing down off a difficult route is most often characterized by a finely tuned sense of alertness to possible mistakes or potential danger. It is always the most dangerous part of a day, and hazards lay in wait to strike at the unattentive.

We had left one ice screw in place at the luncheon stand on our way up; now John was checking it for security when something very odd occurred: the entire slope around us suddenly seemed to sag and perceptibly drop with a sound that was a cross between a *wham* and a *thomp*. Later we joked about this spot as "Whomp Corners," but the immediate concern was to get the hell out of there as rapidly as possible. A rappel was established after a debate about whether a second pin was warranted, but we were sufficiently unnerved by what was probably no more than a settling of recent snow on the ice slope (we later speculated that the event may have been a foreshock of an earthquake) that we decided against doing anything that might cause any further sagging. We knew besides that we would need all the screws we had in making the final relay in the morning.

Roskelley went down first, Gary next, and I, as the eldest, seemed to be accorded the privilege of descending last. As John rappeled out of sight, Gary and I felt a second and lesser *whomp* and I was quickly convinced the whole summer had somehow been a mistake. Going down last was one of the more lonely moments of my life.

We descended the ice in a series of rappels, leaving one fixed rope of 150 feet at the steepest top section. The next day we would go up that rope by means of jumar ascenders in order to bring up our heavy relay loads. We cleared the avalanche gully just before a small but potentially fatal discharge of rock from the hanging ice face scoured the chute, and we then eased down the remaining ice on the confidence of our crampon points and the sense of reprieve that comes at the end of a day of extended pressure.

Marts had observed our progress virtually the entire day and said it was fairly spectacular to watch. He wondered why we seemed to be hurrying through our rappels until we described the spooky moment at "Whomp Corners."

Another great meal, this time a stew of fresh vegetables and chopped Russian salami, seasoned with dried American soup stock. John had prepared this in a pressure cooker, America's answer to the high-altitude fuel shortage. Before we got started on the main course, we finished the last few precious drops of Dewars with slices of Boris, our dried Russian salmon, who was finally reduced to a forlorn skeleton halfway up the north face.

Assuming the weather and the fixed rope anchor at "Whomp Corners" held, we were convinced we could push on through with all our loads and be in striking position for the summit within two or three days at the most. Apart from a slight sense of uneasiness generated by the settling of the snow above the big ice slope and the accumulated fatigue of several days of continuously hard carrying, we were in very high spirits on the eve of our final carry onto the upper face.

Marts had benefited by the rest. Although he was still not back to normal, we thought he would gain strength on

Descent

Ascent

IV 16,700

Escape route

III 15,400

II 13,200

North Edge

I 12,300

North Face
PEAK NINETEEN

the way up. Our other and by now routine worry was the weather as again the sheet of clouds settled from the northwest and the rain came. We were getting used to being four in the Bauer tent, but it was certainly not a matter of preference.

Despite the drizzle, we waited until the last minute to settle into the tent; we were rewarded with the sound of a multi-engined propeller-driven aircraft passing from east to west, seemingly from the direction of China. Soon we could see lights moving through the faintly sunlit cloud breaks, just 2,000 or 3,000 feet above the mountaintops. A few moments later we heard the unmistakable *whoosh* of jets and, again in the breaks of the clouds, caught glimpses of two delta-winged planes, which we imagined were Soviet fighters, flying tight formation on a northwesterly course behind the larger aircraft. We speculated it might have been an electronic surveillance craft with its fighter escort checking out the Chinese border. Life on one of the world's tenser, more spectacular frontiers.

We were up and cooking breakfast early on the 22nd after another night punctuated by ice avalanches roaring off the north face. Our original "classic" route had collapsed even more. The center of the lower ice wall had discharged great sections. The real problem above consisted of the unpredictable combination of time, weather, and the condition of the slope. We had begun to think in hardheaded logistical terms. Weather determined the length of time we could spend above Camp II. Food was time. We had about seven days' rations for the face. We needed only three. Weather also determined the condition of the slope and the speed with which we could get through the various sections of difficulty before it became impossible to pass. There were no other factors we could think of at the moment. We fairly charged out of Camp II for the ice face and Camp III.

We moved through leads with the heaviest loads we

could manage for such terrain. There is no sense of freedom like breaking clear of the base of a mountain and
coming to grips with its real problems. We were all together now, and Marts was going well with a big load. We
hurried through the avalanche gully and found the steep
traverse somehow tougher than before. The ice face was
the same very hard water ice, deceptively steep; it was
even more unfriendly than the ice falls that tumbled down
on either side. Fortunately we were able to pick up everything in the cache and we could go straight through to
Camp III in one last carry.

We jumared up the steepest part on the rope we had
fixed at "Whomp Corners" with no small awareness of the
uncertain layer of snow over water ice menacing above.
We had hardly forgotten the sickening drop of snow some
eighteen hours before. Although our loads were substantially heavier than the day before, jumaring made it all just
manageable. Jumars on less than vertical fixed ropes must
be very positively engaged as one moves up. The very
heavy loads tended to rotate us away from the most effective down-pulling position for the jumars and, combined
with the great gulf of exposure below, made the ice face
more incompatible than ever. We wondered how we got
up that the day before with reasonably heavy loads and no
fixed rope. A good part of the answer was Roskelley—he
had done a great lead the first time.

We reached the anchor platform about noon. Marts, now
feeling much better, was delighted to be well up in the
mountain. The midday sun burned through the intermittent gathering of mist and clouds that trapped the solar
radiation. The heat was exhausting, and we moved slowly
up toward the Camp III cache. We were now threading the
long overhanging crevasses of the middle north face. What
had been rain below for the past five days had built up into
a sizable accumulation of new snow between the crevassed ledges. Our tracks of the day before were covered,

and we regarded the final ice slope with considerable apprehension. If the snow covered the ice to a depth of more than six inches, we were in serious trouble. However, so far as we could tell, the new snow was sloughing off the steep face.

Gary and I took turns breaking trail, and at about 3:00 P.M., we arrived at the cache. We shoveled out a tent platform, and, as Roskelley arrived with the Bauer tent in his pack, Camp III was established. It was an airy scenic spot, and several new summits appeared in the east and west. Because Peak Nineteen is a frontal peak of the range, the real depth and dimension of the Pamirs cannot be appreciated from the north side. I started dinner, and Gary and Roskelley moved out with light loads to reconnoiter the route ahead to Camp IV. They figured to climb another hour and establish a cache at or near the last campsite on the face. We wanted to get as close to the ice face as possible for the last push. Even so, that left a bit less than 3,000 feet of 60- to 70-degree blue ice.

In an hour and a half Gary and John returned, having found a straightforward route to Camp IV. Dinner had, meanwhile, evolved into a simple freeze-dried undertaking, and we had some sproats, cheese, and tea ready for John and Gary as they returned. Marts had come through in good shape, and his morale was greatly uplifted by the day's performance. Head and toe again as four sleeping bags forced all other gear to the outside. We were tiring of all sleeping in the Bauer, but since Camp III was clearly a one-night stand, it didn't seem worth the effort to pitch the two-man lightweight.

More snow in the night; but on July 23 it broke clear as we awakened, and we got off early and fast for Camp IV. Because of the relay the previous afternoon, we could carry the fairly heavy remainder of Camp III straight through.

CHAPTER SIX

▲

Earthquake, Avalanche, and Despair

Carrying in the now deep snow was increasingly tiring, and the morning of July 23 was unusually warm. We floundered up to our waists in places. This was the nastiest work of the expedition thus far. We gasped moving up with our loads and intermittently seemed to drowse in our steps. We could not recall ever being more uncomfortable from heat and a kind of lassitude at such a modest altitude. At last a fairly steep rise, giving way to a gentle slope whose snow alternately held us up then collapsed, and we could see we were almost at the foot of the ice slope.

We considered the alternatives for the Camp IV site, and all simultaneously agreed on a spot under the bulge of two ancient collapsed seracs. We were somewhat to the left of the main ice face, and probings of the slope around the tent platform area indicated settled, stable snow. We dug the platform to accommodate our two tents. Until Camp IV, the four of us had sandwiched into the Bauer Himalayan tent because of the need to keep dry. The tents were originally designed for two, while sleeping three fairly comfortably. Four good-sized climbers went beyond the designer's original intention. But because we had only one waterproof tent fly (actually our vinyl melt tarpaulin) for the two tents, and because it had been storming rain or wet snow all the way from Base, we had found it quite necessary to somehow squeeze all four of us in the Bauer Himalayan tent. It proved unexpectedly tolerable, save when someone occasionally had to relieve himself in the middle of the night, thereby unscrambling three other soundly sleeping mates.

But we had had enough of four in one tent, and besides, we were almost at 17,000 feet, and the oxygen demand in close quarters would be that much greater. The second tent, a Bauer ultralightweight, was more a bivouac tent, but really not bad for two, so long as one had plenty of storage space outside. Gary and I found ourselves in the spacious Bauer Himalayan, and in the smaller tent were Roskelley and Marts.

The cached loads were brought up from a short distance below in a single carry by Gary while the rest of us dug in and set up the camp. I never ceased to be impressed with Gary's quiet, constant strength. We were all terrifically excited to be where we were.

Later in the morning of July 23 at Camp IV, the air became even more oppressive. Huge cumulonimbus thunderheads boiled up from the Alai Valley all the way east into the desolate brown distance of southwestern China. Even at 16,700 feet the air seemed heavy. We had dug a spacious tent platform, with our minds on the gathering squall line (it had begun then to seem like more than a characteristic summer thundershower), and our bodies reacting to the lassitude brought on by the still heat in that momentary, glowing glacial oven.

The platform was on a slope of perhaps 35 degrees. We had probed the slope above and to the sides of the platform to determine snow stability. There had been perhaps

125

twelve to fifteen inches of snow in the past two days of afternoon squalls. We had, in fact, climbed up and down through some of that on our relays. There were no sloughing slides even as we broke through to our waists on our way up from Camp III. All in all, because of that and the lack of any slides from above, the snow seemed quite stable at Camp IV. However, when we were in our respective tents a few minutes after noon, we heard a thundering boom from the direction of the big hanging glacier on the northwest shoulder of Peak Nineteen.

Gary was closest to the side of the tent on which the avalanche let go, and looking out the partly opened vestibule, he could see the huge mass breaking off the ice cliffs. He shouted, "Holy Christ, you won't believe it!"

By the time I got onto my knees and peered over Gary's shoulder, there were still sizable pieces breaking off the face of the ice cliff, but the main mass had pulverized into a huge blend of ice blocks and dust and, gathering more material in the form of seracs and surface snow, it was churning and roaring down through the ice fall on the upper west side of the north face and billowing directly toward our tent, though somewhat on the right diagonal.

It was an enormous thing, traveling at great speed with a sustained grinding and roaring as all the ice pulverized in the kinetic energy of its stupendous force. When an ice cliff segment of a hanging glacier breaks loose, there can be as much material as a solid wall of ice 100 or 200 feet high, 100 feet wide by 30 to 50 feet thick—anywhere from 25,000 to 100,000 tons traveling at speeds upward of 150 miles per hour.

The avalanche kept coming and coming, and all this was happening in the course of 30 to 40 seconds. In such a situation, even catastrophe becomes a subject for reflection and fascination. There was nothing one could do, no place to go. By this time Roskelley and Marts had their heads out and were looking up and back, spellbound yet very scared. Just as the billowing cloud of snow came up and over our tents, we realized the main body of the avalanche had turned off to the left down the main north face. We finally heard it roar out below onto the moraines we had traversed days before. The snow and ice dust settled on our tents for another fifteen or twenty seconds.

We were shaken. We didn't at that point really know how far away it had turned down the face, for it was snowing hard again and we were not particularly inclined to go out on that slope and find out.

It was lunchtime and we were assembled to eat in the Bauer. Lunch was not complicated, but since we had perspired a lot carrying up and making camp, we decided a fairly salty soup and some Dutch cheese plus a lot of Wyler's lemonade were in order.

Between 12:30 and 1:00 P.M. I kicked the tent wall, because the snow load in the midday storm was building. As I did so, the whole mountain began to shake. Although we didn't immediately acknowledge it, we knew we were in a big earthquake. We had read of the earthquakes in Uzbekistan and Kirghizia which had destroyed villages throughout history, but this one was here with us, real; and if we had been greatly frightened and upset by the avalanche moments before, now we were all genuinely fearful.

After I kicked the tent wall, Ullin quietly, but with feeling, said, "Jesus, what *is* this?" I couldn't say anything; I couldn't believe what was happening, and I think we all honestly suspected the whole mountain might fall and take us with it. We simply stared back at each other. There was a feeling that at any moment our whole camp might go tumbling down the ice cliffs just below us. It was a moment of unspoken terror. While it lasted (perhaps five or six seconds), I had the sensation of being suspended in air with the surface oscillating underneath.

We were very quiet for some time. Gary finally announced what we all knew: we had just experienced an earthquake, and John Marts noted that it had been pretty strong, and Roskelley broke softly into an anti-Vietnam war song that soon had us actually giggling. "One, two, three, four, what in the hell are we fighting for; we're all going to die!" We had an argument about whether it had been sung by Elton John, Country Joe and the Fish, or some other outfit; but we all seemed to agree that it had been recorded at Woodstock and that it was not inappropriate to our situation. We began to relax a bit, but we were all in the grip of an uneasiness that did not subside until days later.

Strangely, the earthquake did not bring the mountain down on us, though we heard large avalanches in the distance through the snowstorm. It was at that same moment our friends on Krylenko Pass were in serious trouble. We did speculate about what might be happening to them and were later relieved that in the evening radio transmission there was no sign of emergency.

The afternoon passed slowly, with intermittent but heavy snow showers. The cloud masses during infrequent breaks appeared more ominous than they had in the morning heat. We got out during the pauses in the storm and checked the slopes around camp for stability but could find nothing out of order. The surface snow and older layers all seemed quite stable. Camp IV had nonetheless become a very spooky place. Gary, our most inventive and frequent dinner chef, decided we had had enough trauma for the day and that it was only appropriate that we have a super special meal that evening.

We had a lot of food at Camp IV on July 23. Our relays had been heavy and we were in an exceptionally strong position in terms of equipment and rations. Our food was roughly half Russian and half American.

Food had been the subject of controversy and skepticism within the expedition. Some felt that freeze-dried food had little nutritional value, and one of the climbers even maintained it caused piles. Nevertheless, most of what we brought from the U.S.—a total of twelve man-days per man —was freeze-dried. As it turned out, the last American pork chop, the last item of freeze-dried food, was consumed in Base Camp the day before the teams returned to Moscow.

The Russian food, though on the heavy side, was nutritious and good. The combination of Russian and American rations provided one of the better expedition diets any of us had experienced. Gary had become quite adept at mixing menus in an interesting way, so that we might have one or two freeze-dried items plus boiled fresh Russian vegetables, or a Russian meat dish and American dehydrated vegetables.

Dinner on the night of July 23 was one of these mixed affairs, with red caviar for a starter, followed by Astro eggs and then a steak and a half per man, served with green peas and almonds. By the time we got to the frozen strawberries, we weren't sure we could get through that sumptuous dessert. We decided a chess game was in order. Gary and I were black and Marts and Roskelley white. Marts turned out to be a very formidable opponent, and Ullin and I were quickly dispatched.

We were unusually sleepy and barely able to stay awake for the 9:00 P.M. radio transmission. The snow continued to fall heavily and we realized we were no longer in a series of intermittent squalls; we were in a real storm.

Thunder had been rolling around the horizon toward China all afternoon and evening, and at midnight we heard Roskelley shout something about "There's a war going on over there." As we awakened, we became aware of an enormous lightning storm to the north and east of us. It truly appeared to be some kind of artillery battle or perhaps a vast bombing going on. The Chinese and the Russians? The storm which had held us seemed to have pulled back to the west; the storm born in China seemed to be advancing as a black wall, moving westward down the Alai Valley toward our section of the Pamirs. As it moved toward us, thunder was as continuous as the flashes and getting disturbingly close. When it had reached an estimated five miles' distance an hour or so later, it suddenly veered to the north and west. We slept uneasily into the morning.

It continued to snow into midmorning on the 24th and then became warm again, clearing, and we got a glimpse of the Achik Tash Valley and Base Camp and the main Alai Valley. Everything was thoroughly covered with snow, all the way down into the Alai Valley, perhaps as low as 9,500 feet. We piled out of our tents happily, thinking we could reorganize our equipment left outside, dig a snow cave for safe storage and possible emergency shelter, and prepare our loads, technical gear, and ropes for the summit attempt on July 25.

The final ice slope above us looked eminently feasible and we were already thinking of Base Camp, a hot shower, a couple days' relaxation, and going up the Krylenko face to the east side of Lenin. We had pretty much ruled out a carry up and over the summit of Peak Nineteen and down the west ridge onto Krylenko Pass as too beset by unknowns. We would do the face direct, return to camp, and go off by the northeast shoulder.

Digging the snow cave (not so much for shelter as for auxiliary storage space) was welcome exercise after 24 hours of inactivity. Between turns digging and carrying snow, each man got his personal gear ready for the climb on the 25th. After four hours of relative clearing, the clouds closed in and the snow began again in earnest. During all the preceding days of snow, the final ice slope had remained largely free of any surface build-up, and we had been very hopeful that we could pretty much frontpoint directly up it to the rock bands near the top. By the morning of the 24th, we were disappointed to notice that the face was not completely sloughing its new snow. Now it was snowing again late in the afternoon of the 24th. If much more fell on that face, we would have to wait another day. We briefly considered digging the snow cave out sufficiently to provide a bombproof shelter in which to wait

130

out the weather, but gave it up in favor of conserving energy for the climb. Also, staying in the tents we could keep a much closer watch on the weather and on the slopes.

We felt the camp was doubly secure. We had repitched the tents following the snow build-ups, had stored the substantial supplies of food and climbing gear in the snow cave, and made up our packs for the summit climb in the morning. We were not optimistic about conditions for an early morning departure. It was snowing steadily with little wind. Dinner was another elaborate production, but without the euphoria of our first night in Camp IV. Just before dinner, which Marts and I collaborated on, we checked the snow slopes to the sides and above Camp IV for stability.

We decided to break in on the 8:00 P.M. radio transmission instead of our assigned 9:00 network in order to gain an additional hour's sleep. We did so with the usual "Sasha Three to Bahza. Okay, out." Nothing seemed to be stirring elsewhere on the radio network and we were ready to get five or six hours of sleep. Our plan was to get up at 2:00 A.M., cook breakfast, and get off by 3:30 or 4:00 A.M., a little before first light. We would use the headlamps to get out on the final ice face, make the climb by a reasonably early hour, come back down, pick up camp, and go off the mountain via the northeast ridge by midafternoon.

Gary Ullin's diary, written on July 23 and 24, gives an added perspective to life at Camp IV:

JULY 23, TUESDAY
Heavy clouds at 5:00 a.m. but clear by 6:00. Granola, hot chocolate, F.D. plums and coffee for breakfast. Loaded heavy we carried to 16,700 camp in one trip. I went down and picked up cache. Route went straight up from camp past ice wall and weaved right and left through ice walls to base of headwall. Platform cut out of slope below 30-ft. ice wall. Both tents pitched to give more space. Very hot sun and fast building Cumulo clouds set stage for exciting afternoon.

After drying things and tanning in extremely intense sun we were forced into tents by hail and fog. Thunder and lightning and then a thunder-like CRACK above and to our right which turned out to be a big ice cliff starting down. It multiplied its size as it blasted over a huge serac and fanned out toward us as it funnelled down the central face. It was big and we were freaked. Wind and powder drifted over our tents as the shattered tons crashed to rest below. Then, while we digested our lunch again and reconsidered what the hell we were doing here, the thunder started blasting away again and hail pounded on the tent. In the midst of all the noise I was trying to cut up a bacon bar and Craig was kicking hail off the tent and the ground (snow) under us started shaking. It lasted for maybe two seconds. I looked at Marts and his eyes were as big as mine. I don't like it here so well at the moment and really look forward to base camp and green meadows and hot showers and perhaps a letter from my friend in Seattle. It's 3:40 p.m. and snowing quite hard. If we ever finish this route it will have been a fine climb, a good adventure and a 1st ascent. It has been much warmer than we were led to expect and consequently we have been carrying a lot of éxtra weight in clothing. To replace nervous energy and divert our attention a steak dinner —1½ steaks each, rice and peas, leeksoup, Philadelphia cream cheese and Rye Krisp and F.D. strawberries, jello and graham crackers. Nice.

WED. JULY 24
Snowed all night and continues in the morning, 18 inches new snow as clouds break and hot sun burns in for several hours before afternoon cumulo nimbus blast in again. Now at 7:00 p.m. it's snowing again. I started a snow cave around noon and we completed it to storage size for our gear. The face above appears to have sluffed the new snow and so we hope for good weather and an early start tomorrow.

I first awakened at about midnight. It is an old fly fisherman's and mountaineer's habit to be able to awaken virtually at will at all hours of the night and early morning in pursuit of God knows what, but early on that morning it was snowing hard, and I felt a dull sense of apprehension as I went back to sleep. The snow was not letting up and there were 3,000 feet of blue ice above us. I awakened later, noting the time to be about 1:00 A.M., got partly out of my sleeping bag, opened the tunnel entrance of the tent, and looked out. Still snowing—another six to eight inches of new snow since dinner.

I wakened Gary, described the situation, and said, "We've got to forget it, Gary. We're not going to go up today; we're just going to have to hope this goddamned storm eases up so we can get off this mountain."

Gary sighed, obviously disappointed, and said, "Well, let's check it again at two-thirty or three. I sure wish we could get the hell out of here! This place gives me the creeps. We can't stay on this face in this storm much longer."

The storm made it relatively warm in the tent that night. As I returned to sleep, I kept my right arm outside the sleeping bag. I was sleeping on my left side, facing toward the uphill side of the slope, Gary for the first time was sleeping with his head at the same end of the tent, and he too slept on his left side closest to the uphill side of the tent. His head was well up into the tent corner, as we had stored all the food, cooking gear, stove, and fuel bottles in the opposite end; his knickers and down sweater served as a pillow. Gary tended to sleep rather soundly, as did Marts. Roskelley and I slept fairly lightly.

We must both have slept very soundly during the next 30 to 45 minutes, for the next thing I remembered was a kind of hissing in my ears, a shout from the other tent, a kind of popping as the tent collapsed over Gary and me, and the building up of an enormous weight on my body as the avalanche engulfed our tent platform.

My first thought was that we were definitely in an avalanche and it was carrying us down the slope and into the crevasses below. That was followed almost immediately

by the realization that we simply were buried in the tent
and that I could not move. My right arm was across my
face, and the avalanche had rolled me partially onto my
back. I was totally, frighteningly immobilized and under
enormous pressure. You are going to die! was the only
thought at first.

It was incredibly still. The only sound I could detect
apart from my racing heartbeat was an occasional soft
thump as the snow of the avalanche settled and set into
what seemed concrete hardness. I had an air pocket of
perhaps four or five inches in front of my face, created by
my free right arm outside the sleeping bag. My first reaction was a tremendous sensation of claustrophobia and a
feeling of This is ridiculous. It's not supposed to end this
way, but this seems to be it! Somehow, this is not the
dream of the airliner crashing. This is the crash . . . and
you are in it!

I began calling out to Gary, who should after all have
been not more than one and a half to two feet away. There
was no sound. I tried again and again, saying, "Gary, if you
are there, make some sound against the tent with your
hands." Nothing. Perhaps he was alive but pinned so as to
be unable to move. Then why no voice sound? This was
very bad.

I could move my right arm a little, but any movement
made me gasp and use more air than I suspected I should.
It was becoming evident that with as much snow as
seemed to be covering us, there had to be a limited supply
of air in the envelope of the tent. Judging by the small
pocket created by my arm, there was perhaps 30 minutes'
worth. How can you calculate that sort of thing when you
have no way of knowing the total dimensions of the remaining air space? My estimate of 30 minutes almost immediately seemed ridiculous—I could have an hour or ten
minutes, for all I knew.

I could almost taste panic; the thought of making a desperate effort to push the snow off us, even though I might black out in the process, was tempting. From another part of my mind there seemed to be an insistent, quiet voice that said, Calm down, boy; you can get out of this mess, but you have got to stay cool! If I could hold on, perhaps the two Johns if they had survived would be able to get free and dig Gary and me out. If they hadn't survived the avalanche—well, that was one of the things I was not going to consider. But Gary? What had happened to him? The thought that he had not survived the avalanche was almost inconceivable. Still, there wasn't the slightest sound and he couldn't be more than two feet away.

I decided that my only hope was to try to achieve something like a state of "Zen suspension," or perhaps the lowered tension and breathing levels claimed by adherents of various forms of meditation. Whatever it was and however it was done, I needed to find out in a hurry.

I called again to Gary. I pleaded with him to answer, but realized I was gasping again and slowly forced myself to reduce my rate and depth of breathing. As I tried not to focus on our predicament, I could not avoid thinking of my life, my children, Carol, my family, and friends. It was hard to separate sleep and dream from the sudden overwhelming fact of the avalanche. There was the vague sense that I had heard a shout as the snow came over the tent. Could Roskelley or Marts have been trying to warn us? Could the slide have carried their smaller, lighter tent down the mountain? Don't even think about that. The thought process was quite random. A thought in one direction and then another. There was no sense of serenity—just a dull nagging sense of futility, but an equal sense of stubbornness that I had to stay alive, to find a way out.

I reflected that all in all I had been very lucky in my life and that if this was to be the end of it I could accept the fact. Almost simultaneously I chided myself for allowing such resignation to take over. I felt a flicker of anger at the

135

circumstances after all the work and effort to put the expedition together. How had we gone wrong? We had sited the camp prudently and constantly checked for avalanche danger. Should we have gone off to the northeast ridge the afternoon before? No. No one had ever given it a thought. Had there been another earthquake or an aftershock triggering a slide on an otherwise stable slope? We would never know.

I had reduced my breathing and my sense of complete consciousness, but I felt I hadn't completely lost my sense of time and I estimated we had been buried perhaps fifteen to twenty minutes. The thought of so much time and no sound of Marts and Roskelley and no movement or sign from Gary aroused a new sense of consciousness: I might be the only one left. The thought of being conscious of my death, of slipping away bit by bit, dying without some kind of effort to escape, was equally difficult to accept; and despite the danger of consuming my remaining oxygen too rapidly, I decided to hang it all on trying in some way to cut my way out.

I knew my Swiss Army knife was in my knickers pocket under my head, probably within reach of my right hand, if I could push my hand far enough ahead through the density of the consolidated snow. How to get the knife open and how to use it to somehow cut my way out was very uncertain. How much snow covered us? If there were two and a half or three feet, maybe I could get an arm out before my energy gave out; if it was deeper, I doubted I could do much. It felt as if there might be three feet or more covering us. How to get a start?

I had begun to doubt that the others had survived the avalanche. I could move my right arm back and forth in the shell I had created over my face. I managed to press my right arm ahead to the point of reaching into my pants pocket and slowly extricating my knife. Then I had to push my elbow enough to insert my arm under the flap of my sleeping bag and thread my right hand down to my immo-

bilized left hand. I managed this strange maneuver somehow and, holding the knife in my left hand, I was able to
pull out the large blade with my right fingers and then
move it up through the bag and into a cutting position
within the narrow shell created by my right arm.

It suddenly dawned on me that if the snow was solidly
set up by the avalanche, to cut my way out through God
knows how much depth above would mean the immediate
sacrifice of what little air space remained to me. What to do
with all that snow? I had reached the most despairing moment of that somber night, for I had really begun to doubt
that the two Johns had survived, and now there was little
or no practical hope of getting out on my own. I thought for
a brief moment of willing myself to sleep. Struggle was
obviously useless; my last exertions with the knife convinced me the air pocket was rapidly going stale.

I felt pressure suddenly against my feet; a muffled voice
was calling, "Gary, Bob, are you okay?" and I thought,
Good Lord, we're going to get out! More digging, and I felt
fresh air coming in along the right side of the sleeping bag
and I could hear more clearly John Roskelley yelling for us
to answer; I could feel the frantic digging in the snow at
the foot of the tent. What an incredible feeling of freedom
where there had been moments before so little hope!

I screamed, "I'm okay. Get Gary; I can't hear him! Get
Gary; he's on your right!"

Roskelley replied, "Okay, Bob. You're going to be all
right; we'll get Gary right now."

I heard John Marts in a muffled voice say, "Oh, Jesus!
Gary's really in deep."

Roskelley said, "Dig, John, but don't freeze your hands."
Marts had no gloves and was digging with his sweater covering his hands but not very adequately. As they dug on
Gary's side of the collapsed tent, I felt the pressure on my
left side gradually lessen and I could more clearly hear the
labors and efforts of Marts and Roskelley as they got closer
to Gary. They had his side of the tent fairly well uncovered

and my right arm began to feel free enough to move in the new space. There was a brief debate about cutting the tent fabric. I reached out with my right arm, only inches, and touched Gary. There was no movement or response. He was very still. The back of his head and his neck felt very cold. Then I could feel and hear both Johns cutting through the tent and reaching in to extract Gary. They got hold of his arms and torso, but couldn't seem to free his upper body. His head was wedged deeply in the upper right corner of the tent; the snow outside the tent seemed to have compacted around his neck and head, and they couldn't dislodge him entirely. I reached across and pulled his head by the hair to free it from the snow that encased the collapsed tent surrounding his face. It came free, and the neck seemed somehow distressingly limp as they pulled Gary's body through the split in the tent.

What this suggested did not occur to us at that moment: his neck may have been broken by the force of the avalanche. It had now been so long; Gary was clearly unconscious. When they had pulled Gary's body from the tent John Marts began mouth-to-mouth resuscitation, pumping violently into Gary's lungs. This went on for ten to fifteen minutes, Marts furiously breathing into Gary, trying to ignite some spark of life.

He cried out, "It's just no use; the goddamn air in his lungs is stale! He's dead!"

I felt the two Johns pull Gary's body farther out from the uphill side of the tent and then resume digging in the center and right of my body. The immense weight of the snow seemed gone. I was saved; it was at the worst a bad dream. But Gary was dead and the sudden sadness was overwhelming. The brutal fact of Gary's death mixed with the agony of those long minutes of burial left little more than numbness. I wanted to weep and I simply wanted to be out of the tent. A debate again ensued concerning cutting the tent on my side. Marts, deeply involved in procuring the equipment, maintaining it, and seemingly

138

concerned with returning it safely to the States, felt it would be unwise to cut the tent in a second place to get me out. As I lay in my now largely uncovered portion of the tent remembering they had cut Gary out of his section, the argument seemed singularly unpersuasive. I knew John Marts wanted to preserve the tent, but I also knew the tent and poles had been literally destroyed and it had been slit on the other side. Roskelley seemed to sense the situation from my perspective and shouted, "For Christ's sakes, John, let's cut the goddamned tent. Bob is still alive in there!"

I was just about to suggest exiting through the hole cut for Gary, which would have been the most logical move, when Roskelley, who had cleared the last snow from over my head, cut a slit in the fabric above my head. As he did so we all heard an eerie, terrifying sound. From above and seemingly some distance away, a strangely metallic, whining grinding rumble bore down upon us, and almost simultaneously I heard both Johns cry out in dismay, "Oh, no! Look out, here it comes!"

And then, in unquestionably the most despairing and hopeless moment of my life, I was buried again, snow flooding in through the slit in the tent as I lay facing up on my back, my right arm again partially covering my face, but not so effectively, for this time the air pocket seemed smaller and the weight of snow seemed, if anything, heavier.

I thought, My God, this is really it! Somebody really wants me up there. The others *must* have been carried down in *that* slide. There is no way I can get out of this one!

I felt more deeply buried than before, and the left side of my chest ached as if some of my ribs had been cracked. Snow was now inside the tent and enveloped my face, but somehow my right arm and hand had been in position to create an air pocket again.

The sense of despair and hopelessness seemed complete. Hadn't we lost enough? Gary was dead, we had all been buried once, and now this! It was so desperate and ridiculous that amusement almost flickered across my mind.

It had really been only a matter of seconds, then I heard the muffled voice of Roskelley calling, "Bob, are you okay? We'll get you out, Big Daddy."

Probably 40 seconds to a minute had gone by since the second avalanche came down. Near-death and resurrection twice within 30 minutes.

Marts and Roskelley had nearly uncovered all the snow over me the first time, cut a slit in the tent, and were about to help me crawl out, when they had heard the second avalanche. Rather than trying to jump out to the side or simply trying to brace themselves against the downward flow, they had jumped into the hole left when they removed Gary's body, then backed up into the avalanche.

They couldn't have gained more than one or two feet, if that, but they caused the snow of the avalanche to flow around their bodies. It wasn't a large slide, depositing no more than two and a half to three feet of snow on me, but they avoided being swept off their feet and into the system of crevasses below.

They quickly dug me out, and I crawled through the previously cut slit in the tent out into the wreckage of our camp. Roskelley and Marts hugged me. I was suddenly aware I was only in my thermal underwear and socks.

It was snowing hard, and I couldn't see any sign of the others' tent. I had found my flashlight at the head of my sleeping bag and I moved the beam over what had been camp. It was now only an irregular mound of avalanche debris with a small portion of tent showing where I had escaped. Gary's body had been buried again in the second avalanche. Save for the disordered lumps that marked the violence of the past hour and a quarter, the campsite looked very much as we had first found it. Roskelley was anxious to get away from camp and to a safer site. The situation was clearly desperate. We had nothing left . . . our tents were gone, all our equipment and clothing buried. The storm seemed to have intensified; the whole mountain sounded as if it were avalanching. It had grown bitterly cold.

Marts moved out, following Roskelley up and to the right toward the bergschrund formation we had planned to pass on our way to the final ice slope of the north face. It seemed the only place left to us with any kind of protection from the stream of slides sloughing off the ice face. I remained in the wreckage for a few moments as the others started up the slope. John Marts was stunned; he had no gloves and no boots, and he said he thought his hands and feet were freezing. Before leaving the campsite, I reached back into the slit and dragged out my sleeping bag as well as my knickers. I pulled my heavy down parka out and, in rummaging around at the head of my bed, uncovered the Russian radio we had been keeping warm under our clothes, and the spare batteries for the set. Knowing that Marts and I were without boots and had no chance without them, I rummaged further, finding Gary's boots and mine. Fortunately, we had left the supergaiters on our boots which made them easier to drag along behind.

Dragging the sleeping bag and the two pairs of climbing boots and following up in the rapidly filling-in tracks of Marts and Roskelley, my progress was very slow along the 300 feet toward the schrund. My feet were rapidly turning numb, covered only by a pair of medium weight socks, but there was no time or place to stop and try to pull on my boots. As I climbed, I kept telling myself, This is not happening, the avalanche was a dream, after all. I read about all this somewhere before.

Above I could hear Roskelley digging desperately into the base of the schrund. Marts joined him while I was partway up the slope. By the time I reached them, Roskelley had scooped out a shallow ledge in the granular old snow at the schrund's base, with a low sloping roof overhead. I gave Marts my mitts to dig with.

John Marts dug some more and then we began to settle ourselves in the small half cave. Roskelley and I had more warm clothing on, so we sat on the outside with Marts in the middle. We zipped the bag open and dropped it over our feet and lower bodies. We rapidly became cold and periodically pounded one another to keep our circulation going.

We talked about Gary and what had happened. We were stunned and confused by the avalanche. It was hard to make much sense out of anything, but we felt that each had done pretty much what he had to. Gary, who apparently had died instantly, hadn't had a chance. There were private tears, but no really open sharing of our individual sadness. It was as if, had we all let it out, we might very well lose the little control we had. I remembered the incredible and harrowing night seven of us had spent in two collapsed tents at 24,800 feet on K2, after an avalanche had swept Art Gilkey off the mountain. This night seemed worse, since we had no equipment.

I had become especially close to Gary. We had made plans for the coming winter when he and his girl, Gretchen, would visit me in Aspen. We had many laughs, for Gary had a Walter Mitty-ish view of himself and saw in me a kind of aging romantic. We liked our "Mash" team members, the two Johns, very much, and talked a good deal about other members of the American expedition. It had become evident that we had a special group of people with a great variety of individual personality. But of all that talented group, Gary was a particularly special source of strength and laughter.

At this point, and under those improbable circumstances, we tried to force ourselves not to think about the totally demoralizing fact of Gary's death. It was undeniably there, a sharp pain, but we had to somehow come to terms with our own survival. Subconsciously, we tried to focus on subjects that were immediate and related to the expedition.

We had all speculated to some extent about Marty and Peter and the whole issue of romantic relationships and of women on mixed expeditions. Now, as we shivered increasingly and determined to stay awake so as to avoid frostbite, we found ourselves discussing with curious detachment a subject that is not easily faced under normal, unstressed circumstances. We tended to agree that on a trip such as the Pamirs expedition, representation of women was important, but the big question was how they fitted in with the group as a whole. Marts held the view that women team members should represent the highest possible achievement in feminine mountaineering and that only after that had been determined should their compatibility and cooperative spirit be taken into account. He felt one or two girls from the Northwest had been passed over despite outstanding climbing ability because of their tendency to use gamey language and present a less than "clean-cut" image.

I noted that in Pete Schoening's mind there had been considerable uneasiness about the whole problem of including women at all, and that his feeling was a sincere concern to create the best possible "American image" with the Soviets. When the expedition was about five weeks away from departure and we had selected only one woman, it had seemed fair to predict that we might be criticized for "tokenism." Contacting John Evans, we quickly determined that Molly Higgins might be able to take part on such short notice, and it seemed a reasonable alternative.

My personal feeling was that the closer in mountaineering skills a woman climber was to her male teammates, assuming a solid compatibility factor, the more likely a harmonious effort would result. I believe almost every male member of the expedition felt that women could and should make good team members if, for the duration, they were co-equals in effort.

Probably the best answer was to encourage all-women expeditions and simply avoid the whole damned issue! Perhaps two teams, one male and one female, could approach a summit from opposite directions and have a free-for-all on top. Such sexist thoughts recurred vividly as I would awake from a brief doze, shivering violently, and then a momentary flow of tears as the reality of Gary's death punctuated the now overwhelming cold.

When we had been in our cave an hour or so, we heard a whooshing sound above and an avalanche of spindrift snow poured down over the top of the schrund, pelting our exposed feet in the sleeping bag projected from the cave, and reminding us the margin was very thin indeed. We began to talk of rescue and our chances of getting off Peak Nineteen. The conversations were sporadic and somewhat listless as cold and exhaustion from the avalanches were taking their toll.

Roskelley had suffered quite serious frostbite on Dhaulagiri, the price of a superb and successful summit effort on that 26,810-foot peak. John said he thought his feet were all right, but he took his boots off and we alternately massaged one another's feet. Marts had somehow found his down booties in the wreckage and it seemed his feet were the only warm part of his body.

About 4:00 A.M., a fairly good-sized spindrift avalanche came down, and I thought for a moment it might pluck the sleeping bag away. We were too cold then to be as frightened as we ought to have been.

CHAPTER SEVEN
▲
The Escape from Peak Nineteen

We agreed I would begin a series of Mayday calls to Base at 6:00 A.M. I counted the shaking minutes from about 4:30 A.M. on. Briefly the storm paused and the clouds pulled away from the base of the mountain and the lower Lenin Glacier; the lights of Base Camp sputtered through the snowfall in the new whiteness that covered the Achik Tash out to the Alai Valley as far as Daraut Kurgan. The storm had been total; the war from China the last two nights had been the weather.

By 6:00 A.M. we were dangerously cold. Shivering constantly, soaked through from melting snow, we knew hypothermia had set in. Our teeth chattered to the point where conversation was very difficult. The outside temperature had dropped; it was now far below freezing, probably close to zero Fahrenheit, and it continued to snow fairly hard, driven by a strong wind out of the northeast. We had become listless in the cold. One is conscious of the dangerous torpor of hypothermia and even indifferent to it.

I made my first call to Base from under the roof of our

cave with the aerial extending out of the mouth. "Bahza, this is Sasha Three. Mayday, Mayday, Mayday." I repeated the message several times, but there was no sound from Base. Apparently the Russians weren't monitoring at that hour. This was discouraging, perhaps more because the wind was flooding in directly at the mouth of our semi-cave than because the Russians weren't awake.

Between 6:00 and 7:00 A.M. it seemed to get colder, probably because we ourselves were losing our vital body heat. I remember thinking, If this storm continues and we don't somehow get more clothing and more equipment and even some more food, we are finished! There was simply no way to retreat off the mountain on our route of ascent. It was much too steep and therefore too prone to avalanche, and this increased and enlarged the sense of our being trapped.

Seven A.M. came as we debated the possibility of rescue, and I once again began to transmit the Mayday signals to Base. We had agreed that transmission on the hour made more sense, as we knew the Russians had assigned time segments five minutes before and five minutes after the hours of 8:00 and 9:00 in the mornings and evenings. We didn't know how early the various teams were reporting in, so we had made a blind stab at 6:00 A.M. and were now on again at 7:00 A.M. There was no answer the second time.

At this point, the cold seemed to have taken over our personalities. I remember wondering in a kind of wooden way, Why are we transmitting Mayday when all we need to say is "Bahza, this is Sasha Three . . . Help!" We were stiff, listless, and shaking constantly. We slept some between 7:00 and 8:00 A.M.

At 8:00 A.M. I changed the batteries, replacing those in the puny Russian set with those in the plastic bag I had kept next to my stomach. I began transmitting again from within the cave with the aerial pointing outward toward Base. We heard some garbled sound, and we suddenly began to come alive. Roskelley extracted himself from his part of the sleeping bag and said, "Let me try the radio from the outside."

He took the set and slowly enunciated, "Bahza, this is Sasha Three. Mayday, Mayday, Mayday . . . Do you read?"

After a moment we heard what sounded like a confused Russian voice on the other end responding to Sasha Three, and John said, "Bob, get out here and transmit from in front."

As I left the relative warmth of the sleeping bag's partial covering, I realized how wet I had become on my underside, back, and arms and how really chilled I was. I began shaking violently as I took the set from Roskelley. I added more information to the standard Mayday call.

"We have been avalanched and we are in bad shape. Gary Ullin is dead. Do you read us, Bahza?"

We suddenly heard a voice speaking English, a voice with a slight Russian accent which I quickly recognized as Eugene Gippenreiter's.

"Sasha Three, this is Base Camp. Can you hear us, Sasha Three?"

"Base Camp, this is Sasha Three. This is a Mayday transmission. Do you understand? We are in trouble. Do you read this message?"

Gippenreiter came on again, "Please hold one minute, Sasha Three. Please wait."

In this interval I was shaking so violently I longed to go back under the sleeping bag with the two Johns. But our hopes had risen. At least they knew something was up.

Suddenly an unmistakable voice came on. "Sasha Three from Base Camp. We cannot read you clearly. Please transmit slowly. This is John Evans to Sasha Three. Come in, please."

As I recognized John's warm voice, my eyes filled with tears and with great effort I began transmitting haltingly, slowly, enunciating carefully through chattering teeth.

The feeling of emotion was profound. "John, this is Bob Craig. We have been avalanched. Gary Ullin is dead. He died in an avalanche. We have no gear. We have a small snow cave. We are very cold. We need help. Do you read me?"

There was a pause, then John Evans came on again, "Bob, your voice was garbled. We are not sure we understand the message. We think you said Gary Ullin is dead, but we are not sure. Please press your transmitter button down twice if our understanding is correct; once if we are wrong. Over."

I pressed the button down twice, freezing tears running down my face as I did so. John's voice filled with emotion, the strong, gentle climber came back on: "Sasha Three, this is Base. We understand you, Bob. Gary is dead. We are very shocked and sad, and very much with the three of you at this moment. We have to know how to help you. A rescue team will get under way as soon as possible. Please transmit slowly and tell us if you understand me." As he finished his transmission, he sounded even on our uncertain receiver to be clearly shaken.

I suddenly felt exhausted as well as dangerously cold. I said, "Base Camp. John, it is too cold to transmit any more. We must try to get warm. I will call again at ten A.M. It is good to know you are there. Over and out."

Base Camp acknowledged that our message was understood, and I crawled back into the cave and under the sleeping bag and promptly fell asleep.

The morning became a blur of chilled semi-awareness. We transmitted at 10:00 A.M., aware by then that we were becoming increasingly hypothermic. It continued to snow, but the ambient temperature had risen. We didn't establish much more in our communication, but John Evans did note that they were asking Aeroflot in Dushanbe and Osh to send two helicopters to provide rescue support. We explained in more detail what had happened. They understood.

John Marts said he was going down to the wreckage of the campsite, and I informed him he'd do it over my dead body. He said, "Goddamnit, if we don't get some more clothing and sleeping bags, we'll all die anyway!" I argued the avalanche danger was just too great. It was snowing fairly hard, but it seemed brighter outside.

We dozed again. By 11:30 A.M., it had become quite bright and we could actually feel the warmth of the sun burning through the snow-filled cloud cover. The midday lull in the storm, which we had experienced each of the past two days, had returned. Marts announced flatly that he was going down to camp. We could just make out the area as the sun burned off the cloud cover. The site was marked by two slight irregularities of the tent platform. No equipment showed and there was no sign of our snow cave. There was no further arguing with John. Roskelley and I felt extremely apprehensive about his going down, but we had begun to recognize he was right—we couldn't effectively survive another night without more clothing and protection, not to mention food. We might survive, but we wouldn't have enough strength left to escape off the mountain even if the weather and snow conditions improved.

We all crawled out of the cave at the same time. It had become quite warm, luxuriously warm. We pulled everything we had in the cave to the outside and laid the various items out to dry. Roskelley stood around on one leg and then the other, shared a perfunctory radio call to Base in which we indicated our present status, and finally said, "I've got to go down with John. He can't do it all by himself. We've got to take the chance. You stay here and you can keep in touch with Base."

The thought of our all getting wiped out in one final avalanche was very compelling, and I gratefully accepted Roskelley's subtle perceptions. I felt closer than ever before to Marts, who had proven wiser than I when it counted.

149

The two Johns dug at the sites of both tents and began to uncover vital articles of equipment. Digging with his hands until he found gloves, Marts uncovered the two sleeping bags and the foam pads he and Roskelley had left behind in the avalanche. Roskelley, searching in the Bauer vestibule, found the stove and a fuel container, some food, Gary's heavy down parka, and a spare bivouac sack that was to prove most valuable in the next few hours. They never did locate the storage cave.

As they dug, I spread all the clothing items we weren't wearing—the sleeping bag, mittens, boots—in the now penetrating sunlight. I enlarged the cave some, and looked down at the boys digging among the emerging debris. It just didn't seem possible that it had all happened. I made another scheduled radio call at 2:00 P.M. and learned from Al Steck that a rescue group had set out from Base, led by John Evans and Fred Stanley. We had no idea of the bizarre and terrifying experience Al, John, Fred, and Bruce Carson, not to mention the seven others, had had on the Krylenko face just two days before.

Finally, it was not possible to remain in the cave merely drying out equipment, digging out and enlarging our snow cave, and soaking in the welcome sun. I went down to the tent platform. I was weaker than I had imagined. The scene was remarkable, for the digging of the Johns revealed just how much snow had buried the camp.

I marveled at the fact that anyone survived. We uncovered Gary's body and placed him back in his sleeping bag. His face was serene and revealed no sign of suffering or stress. A small trace of blood showed at the corner of his mouth—internal bleeding following suffocation? We would never know. There was nothing we could do about burial at that point, so the primary effort was to retrieve whatever vital equipment we could that would keep us alive.

The storm clouds had begun to build and consolidate

150

again, and it was clear that we needed to get ourselves settled for the night, to cook some food, and hope for an airdrop and a better day tomorrow. Going back up the slope, I began to feel we were going to survive our ordeal. We had the essentials to get through the next few days until the storm cleared and support could reach us or we could climb down.

The others followed, carrying whatever they could handle in their hands and arms, wearing jackets and excess clothing. The sun had gone and the wind was up; but even though it was beginning to snow lightly, there was still warmth in the air. We took final scoops from the cave. It was still not a full structure, but it was a great improvement from its condition early in the morning. We giggled a little about our new luxury, but the threat was all too evident; exit off the north face of Peak Nineteen was going to be a nightmare. The face had to be one vast avalanche waiting to be released.

We had a 4:00 P.M. schedule on the radio. "Bahza, this is Sasha Three. Come in, please."

The response came in much stronger and clearer than anything we had heard before. "Sasha Three. We are on the North Face Glacier heading for the northeast ridge of Peak Nineteen. How are you doing?"

We recognized the voice as Fred Stanley's; he was one of our quiet, strong ones. I replied, "Fred, it's good to hear your voice. We are okay. We have recovered quite a bit of our equipment, enough to stay alive, but we don't have our climbing gear, since we couldn't find the storage cave. Is there any chance of an airdrop helicopter? Over."

Fred came back on and explained that he and John Evans and a mixed international group were on their way to the northeast ridge to help us off the mountain. He also explained that plans for helicopters were uncertain, but he did understand that the Soviet choppers could lift us off a lower level of the mountain. We cut in that we didn't feel we needed to be lifted off. We mainly needed a shovel for digging out our gear. He suggested we call Base Camp again and that his group would remain silent, monitoring the call. We signaled Base again.

A new American voice came on. It seemed to be Chris Wren, who informed us that two Soviet helicopters had flown into Base Camp from Dushanbe and Osh, and that the plan was to fly a drop over us with the second chopper standing by to lift us off the lower mountain or perform whatever support tasks seemed appropriate; and what did we need?

We replied again that we needed most a shovel to find and dig out the snow cave which had so far eluded efforts by hand. We needed climbing gear—ice axes and a rope in the event we didn't uncover the cave—and we needed two bamboo poles or something similar to mark Gary's body so that we might have a chance at recovery later on.

Chris got back on immediately saying an airdrop would be attempted at 9:00 A.M. tomorrow, the 26th, and that the Russians would try to provide all the requested materials. We established a radio contact for 8:00 A.M.

As we settled in the cave, Marts seemed glum. The tone of his voice suggested that besides the overall situation something else was bothering him, and Roskelley, in his characteristically direct fashion, said, "What's biting you, Marts? You sound miserable. Man, we're in solid now— dry, warm; we've got food, a stove, plenty of extra clothing,

"Sure, John," I broke in. "We're going to make it because we're together and thanks to your disagreeing with me, we've got enough gear to survive and find the rest of it."

It was at that point that we noticed John's eyes as he lay scrunched down in his bag between the two of us. They were virtually swollen shut.

"You're snow blind, aren't you, son?" I said in my most solicitous, avuncular fashion.

"Yeah, goddamnit. I never found my sunglasses down there in the wreck," John replied. "I'll have a hell of a time getting off this mountain."

Roskelley and I communicated our mutual worry without words. Marts had performed well under stress; he had insisted on doing what we had to do against my excessive conservatism, but snow blindness in these circumstances was no trivial thing. I remembered that our medical kit, which had been recovered in the wreck, had an eye ointment.

Using the ointment, we glued John's eyes shut with what was perhaps an overdose. Just the thought that we had the right medication was somehow cheering. We were definitely more comfortable, actually warm in our bivouac, and I got some water going for hot drinks. We had nibbled at food during the day, but had had no real nourishment since dinner the night before. The wind was up, and spindrift slides were coming down from the final ice face over our bergschrund roof and periodically burying the lower portion of our bivouac sack in which the feet of our sleeping bags protruded from the snow cave. It was much colder. It was also clearing, but there was so much blowing snow in the air, one had the impression the blizzard had returned.

The 6:00 P.M. radio schedule would be the last for the day—one more at 8:00 A.M., then the airdrop and then it was anyone's guess. At 6:00 P.M. we got a strong signal from Evans and Stanley. They were moving up the glacier below the north face and had camped for the night, planning to mount the northeast ridge in the morning. They had a long way to go, but then so did we. Base Camp came in and repeated the Soviets' plan to attempt a helicopter drop in the morning. It was Al Steck; his familiar calm, steady voice had the unwarranted effect of making me believe everything would indeed work out.

Now we had two sleeping pads for the three of us and

each of us was in his own comfortable bag. But the cold was palpable, and exposure had taken its toll—we were weaker than we cared to believe. We had hot chocolate, munched on some biscuits, and began to sleep for short intervals. Spindrift poured off the ice in a steady stream which we could not entirely push out of the cave entrance with our feet. Every hour or hour and a half either Roskelley or I had to get out of the bags and with our mittened hands shovel out the entranceway. We were shaken by the total disappearance of our carefully-prepared storage cave, and we had no certainty that the ice face above might not discharge on us, trapping us in our bivouac sack in the miserable cramped cave. If a really big one let go with enough force, it could have sucked us right off the slope. The specter of the steep, overloaded slopes we would have to cross to escape the next day dominated our consciousness as we intermittently dozed.

It was a better night than the night before, but it was still strange. We could not forget that Gary's body lay in his sleeping bag among the ruins of Camp IV. The spindrift continued to approach small avalanche size, and while nothing much was said, a recurring sense of apprehension filled our cramped space. The fact of Gary's death seemed to come and go in waves, and we endlessly asked, "What could we have done?"

Morning seemed never to come. For a time around 3:00 A.M., the spindrift let up and the sky was fairly clear with bright stars, and with the cloud blanket gone it became very cold. We slept uninterrupted for a couple of hours. Marts had been miserable with snow blindness, but at least he had slept some. With the arrival of dawn at about 5:30, we began the long, painful wait for the 8:00 A.M. radio schedule. We could see the lights of Base Camp as daylight began to fill the valley. Clouds reappeared at various levels, but it looked as though the chopper could fly.

I crawled out about five minutes before 8:00. It was

clearly the coldest moment we had encountered on the expedition. I began transmitting early in hopes someone would be listening, and fortunately Steck and Wren were there to hear me stammering through chattering teeth, "Sasha Three to Base." They quickly informed us the chopper would be off at 9:00 A.M. to make a drop attempt. The pilot would have as spotters Peter Lev and Eugene Gippenreiter, and he would make at least one pass to assess the terrain and air conditions. We didn't much envy Peter and Eugene, but their involvement in the operation made things seem much closer, much more personal.

At about ten minutes past 9:00, we heard the distinctive thumping, whirring sound of a helicopter. We searched, looking out from the mouth of the cave, and finally spotted it to the north of us ascending from about 15,000 feet. They had spotted our camp from Base, and Eugene and Peter would guide the pilot in as close as he could maneuver.

Roskelley scrambled out of his sleeping bag and emphatically told me to stay in mine, that he would handle the drop, and that if he needed me, he'd let me know. It didn't take much urging. The chopper stood off from the north face of Nineteen gaining altitude until it was at about 18,000 feet, then approached us at what seemed to be considerable speed, spinning away over our cave to the northwest. They were just looking on that pass. How could they possibly put anything close to us with an approach like that? We called to the helicopter on the radio and got nothing but static. Pete Lev and Eugene were up there. It seemed very incongruous.

The chopper returned, still moving very fast. John shouted, "There's one load! Goddamn—it's above us in that hanging avalanche stuff!" The helicopter veered away for another pass. As the chopper sheared off to the north, it gained more altitude and then came in down the north face fast, then slowing down but keeping full power on the blades, and put the loads in much closer. On that pass he

155

almost grazed the snow, he was so close. Roskelley shouted again. "Wow, I can't believe it—he put them practically on the camp—two of them!" A very brave, incredibly skillful job of flying!

Roskelley had to retrieve the first load that had landed in the precarious spot above the schrund. Nothing big had come down the face, and the slopes around the camp seemed strangely stable; but we still had to find the load with the shovel. Without it, we couldn't locate the snow cave and our climbing gear.

Roskelley forced his way up the steep, deep drifted snow, around the corner of the schrund, and into the exposed, dangerous line of the upper face. Silence. Wisps of spindrift spurting off the schrund. I dreaded the sound of a crack in the snow load over the ice; then, after only about ten minutes, we heard Roskelley coming back. He had the load and the shovel. Another twenty minutes and all three loads were at our bivouac cave.

Even if we didn't find the storage cave, we now had three ice axes and a climbing rope. We could get off. The chopper had dropped us fuel, a stove, water, various items of food, and a pair of cross-country skis to mark Gary's body.

We all descended to the camp and began to try to find the other necessities we badly needed to get down. Roskelley began to dig a grid for the storage cave. Marts was miserable with snow blindness, but gamely assembled equipment. We fortunately found a spare pair of sunglasses for him. John found the cave about 11:00. About seven feet of snow blocked the original entrance. We would not have lived had we taken shelter there, as we had very seriously considered doing the afternoon before the avalanche.

Everything was as we had left it in anticipation of the climb: Gary's pack, meticulously ready. What should we carry down of his personal effects? Not much. We were not nearly so strong as we had been; hypothermia has insidious effects. We decided we must go down that day. The weather at the moment was the best in three days, and though large cloud masses surrounded the horizons, our main concern was to get off the face as quickly as possible before the storm renewed and loaded the face with even more avalanche danger.

The thought of crossing the face to the northeast ridge had haunted us for two days. We had to get out of there—fast. John Marts wondered whether we should wait another day to rebuild our strength and allow the support parties to get into position. After a moment's thought about another night on the face, he agreed we had to get away immediately.

We began to make up our loads, eliminating everything but essentials. We took those personal things of Gary's like his diary and camera that we thought would mean the most to his parents and Gretchen. We dug his body out once again from the spindrift that had covered it by almost eighteen inches. Again, there was the sense that Gary had died without struggle; his face seemed peaceful. We placed an American summit flag over his chest, zipped the sleeping bag tight, and covered him with a layer of about a foot and a half of snow. We marked his resting place with the Soviet cross-country skis.

We moved out shortly after 1:00 P.M., July 26, John Roskelley leading, then Marts, then me. We did not look back as we left camp. It was still and fairly warm; the big storm cloud columns were beginning to build. We estimated we needed two hours to get to the ridge. As we moved slightly down and away from Camp IV, the place we had so happily arrived at three days before, the snow seemed surprisingly stable. It was, nevertheless, deep and therefore worrisome, but Roskelley plunged ahead, machinelike, breaking trail at a steady pace. Though we were carrying only 40 pounds, all our great conditioning had apparently been lost in the recent hours. Marts was miserable, but he said little and was soon to display his good judgment.

The route led up and leftward across the east side of the

face. It was now real work compounded with anxiety: we were directly under a big loaded ice bulge. Ominously quiet. Hot.

We reached a slight ridge crest, safe for a moment, and now a new, important decision. Two possibilities were offered: one, a descending traverse to a cluster of seracs just off the northeast ridge, a long, exposed, but apparently much faster, easier route. The second, ascending right to the main northeast ridge, was definitely more work and probably a little more time consuming. Roskelley wanted to go left, traversing down. I was apprehensive, but I was tired and tempted to go down against my better judgment. Marts settled it. "We can't go down there. That stuff is hanging, just waiting to go; let's go up." That was it, and I think it was at that point we actually escaped from Peak Nineteen. Looking up at the traverse the next day from the lower glacier, we noted that one of the big seracs had toppled and that a large section of the slope we would have had to cross had been wiped clean by an avalanche.

Thirty minutes later we reached the crest of the main ridge. We were safely off the north face. We would get down. The clouds, which had held so fortunately, closed in even as we were establishing a safe route to the lower northeast buttress. As we moved down, we sensed we might wander off course to the right, so we stopped and began taking compass bearings, trying to establish a general line into the saddle below.

Then we clearly heard voices below, and our first elated inclination was to sit tight and let them come to us. We called out, yodeled, whistled, but there was no answering response. We had to keep moving into blind alleys and had to retrace our path to the known line of the ridge. Where were the voices? A complicated network of crevasses, strangely straddling and running parallel to our descending ridge, forced new route findings and decisions.

As we decided to thread it through the maze the longest

and safest way, the mist down in the saddle lifted, and we saw five figures making quite rapid time up toward our line of descent. Very carefully we worked through the crevasses and skirted a couple of half-tumbled seracs. The rescue team came on at a fierce pace, and it seemed to me they had skis on to cover the ground so quickly.

We cleared the last threatening crack in the maze, and our two parties joined. It was a joyous and tearful moment as Fred Stanley, John Evans, and three Frenchmen—Yves, Bernard, and François—embraced us and removed our packs from our backs. Between tears and laughter, I remember wondering how they had come so far so fast.

The Frenchmen and Americans were the advance team of a large rescue support group composed of Soviets, Bavarians, Swiss, West Germans, and Dutch. We were touched to hear how quickly the rescue group organized and learned that John and Fred barely managed to make it on the truck as the group raced out from Base Camp bound for the moraine, that they were not the leaders, and that the Soviets had indeed organized the rescue effort.

What had been opening and closing clouds now became again the continuing storm, with violent blasts of wind and heavy snow. We tied in with the others and raced down off the mountain with no real sense of where we were, only that we were safe. The storm had returned with real violence, and the thought of still being on the face reinforced our sense of thanksgiving. As we descended, there was a blur of figures in the fog and blizzard, warm embraces from men we only vaguely recognized from Moscow and Base Camp, food and a quick medical checkup in a collection of Russian tents at the base of the ridge, and then down again along the edge of the main glacier. We descended until just past dark, finally on easy moraine terraces where the Soviet rescue leaders decided we should camp.

Kostya Kletsko, Master of Sport in Mountaineering, and one of the "coaches," as these top Russian climbers were known, seemed to be in charge of the overall operation. He in turn was backed up on the Soviet side by Oleg Boresenok and Tolia, both also Masters of Sport, and Ivan, one of the doctors from Base. Generous cupfuls of vodka were passed to us as we dropped our loads in the dark, and the Soviets made us understand that they were pitching a tent for us and not to worry. The Bavarians quickly heated some food and we soon felt quite contented both inside and out. The Soviets had pitched their best tent for us and laid their thickest ground pads. We crawled into our bags and fell into exhausted sleep, which for me was only marred later by a nightmare. Something about suffocation. Roskelley shook me awake.

On the morning of July 27, we got off early, eager to get back to Base. We felt stronger; John's eyes fortunately were a little better. As we filed down the dark hummocks, among large boulders and across small surface streams of the moraine, there was a confusion of many tongues echoing along the glacial corridors. French, German, Russian, and Dutch. We had, more by chance of a mountaineering emergency than design, become a truly international gathering.

The morning was mild and intermittently sunny as we proceeded down the uneven terrain of the moraine. I was at the head of the column just behind Kostya Kletsko, who was setting a pleasant pace that took us into a small enclosure rising to a series of rock-strewn morainal mounds. There were small clumps of grass and occasional wildflowers growing on the dying glacier. From the left I saw a fairly large catlike animal walk for several paces from behind one of the mounds, then break into a run, then stop and look over its right shoulder head on at us. As it stopped, I felt a shiver of excitement: it appeared to be a snow leopard—hardly 50 yards away. It stared at the approaching file of men, then went quickly into what appeared to be a lair under a large boulder. I whispered,

"Kostya, panthera?" He winked at me, very pleased, "Da, panthera." We hardly broke stride and continued on past and to one side of the lair. We had seen a snow leopard, a beautiful, powerful creature, russet and beige, perhaps 150 pounds, rare among all animals on the earth—in one of the wildest, most inhospitable corners of the world. Nothing any longer seemed very unusual in the Pamirs.

As we reached the crest of the slope above the moraine at the by now dismantled military camp and the edge of the edelweiss meadow, Pete Schoening came striding down on us, our great strong friend who had known so much tragedy and with whom I had experienced the death of another friend on K2, 500 miles south of us, and said it all with his eyes. No words, just an embrace, and we slung our packs on the waiting military trucks. Michael Monastyrski approached with tears in his eyes. "I told you to be careful, Robert. And now this." We were back on dry ground again, off the glacier and among the flowers; there were again tears and the unlikely sense of returning home . . . in Russia.

Arriving in Base a few minutes later, we experienced the cumulative and strongly final emotion of homecoming. We had virtually exhausted our capacity for tears, though the loss of Gary remained agonizingly real and immediate for the three of us. What we did not appreciate until later was that our teammates had been mourning the loss of Gary for two days prior to our return to Base. We quickly assembled, along with the British, French, Soviets, and a number of other European and Japanese climbers, on the parade before the rank of international flags and conducted a brief service in Gary's memory. The flag was lowered to half staff, Jed Williamson said a brief eulogy to his good friend, and then a moment of silence. The Soviets lowered their flag to half staff, and then for many of us a sense of emptiness came over Base.

The Soviets had been so concerned about conditions following the earthquake and the situation arising out of Gary's death that they had brought up a small contingent of mountain-trained soldiers to assist in manning the camp, and for the possible and hopefully unnecessary task of evacuating injured climbers.

As we had returned, there was a certain sense of embarrassment at overreaction on the part of the Soviets, but what probably went unnoticed was the appreciation by the Europeans and the Americans for their consideration under the circumstances.

We had worked hard and traveled more than halfway around the world to do significant climbs in the Pamirs, yet our first efforts had ended in the death of one of our finest climbers and very nearly in the deaths of fourteen others, distributed among three teams.

Now it appeared that three major objectives of the expedition, probably four, had been wiped out by earthquake, weather, and avalanche in less than ten days. There was no returning to the east side of Lenin and Peak 6852 via Krylenko Pass, and it was doubtful anyone would visit the north face of Peak Nineteen again.

It seemed unlikely Pete would return to the Dzerschinsky Glacier with as much snow as had accumulated. We knew we could run a crocodile string of American climbers up the Razdelny route on Lenin, but the zest of exciting, interesting mountaineering had gone out of the expedition.

The other climbers in Base Camp were very nice in many subtle ways—mostly said in glances. The three of us from Peak Nineteen had developed a special affection for the twenty-five or so climbers who had come up to help us. The affection was vague, as we hadn't gotten to know them well, but it was there. Even the old Italian climbers, who had not gone to Peak Nineteen, had wept on the day of our return. They remembered we had sung La Montanara together. The Russians were embarrassed and extremely kind. One could sense that they felt they had in some way failed. That thought never entered our minds—they had done the best they could under difficult conditions in extremely dangerous mountains.

The Austrians who were not climbers seemed indifferent if not clearly disinterested in what had happened on Peak Nineteen. There were exceptions: an older, overweight, rather nattily attired man grasped my hand and said softly in German, "It makes us very sad, youngster." For the "youngster" appellation, I forgave all the Austrians.

Erika Prokosch, an attractive Viennese physicist of Axt's team, approached us, eyes brimming, and asked if there was anything she could do to help. For those of us who knew her and knew how she had suffered from altitude illness, this gesture had special meaning.

A lot of climbing took place before the earthquake and storm. Two French and two German teams had climbed Peak Nineteen by its northwest ridge. The Scots explored an area of previously unvisited mountains to the east of Peak Nineteen but were prevented from climbing them because they could not establish lines of supply and storage.

Wolfgang Axt did a solo ascent of Peak Lenin and helped several Austrians to the top via the standard Razdelny route before the afternoon squalls matured into a real storm. Several Soviets made high-speed ascents of Lenin, including Vladimir Shataeyev, husband of Elvira, leader of the Soviet women's team. For the most part, though, the various national teams had been using the first week to ten days in doing lesser ascents or getting into position for more challenging routes on various peaks of the Pamirs.

On the whole, no ascents of any great consequence were achieved during this period, though many significant climbs were begun.

During the afternoon of the 27th, Michael Monastyrski undertook to make Marts and me forget Peak Nineteen. He used his entire liquor supply in the process—and, for that matter, probably part of some other Soviet's—as we drank far into the night. The process was momentarily successful, though I discovered the next day (and for the second time) that hangovers at almost 12,000 feet are exceedingly cruel.

Marts, still slightly affected by the flu, was mercifully spared the worst ravages of that evening and retired early and without pain to his tent. Monastyrski and I had started our bout in a low-keyed, philosophical manner, talking first about our respective roles in World War II, how Michael lost his leg in an artillery barrage as he, a lieutenant, commanded a Soviet battery at Kiev, how his career as a climber was shattered by a handful of shrapnel, but how the Soviet Union looks after its heroes for life.

We then discussed the meaning of life and death in terms that became increasingly vague, so that almost without noticing we began to trade quotations from Shakespeare, Wordsworth, and Dylan Thomas, trying with decreasing success to focus on ultimate themes.

Somewhere, about mid-evening, among the great issues of life from which love was not missing, Michael decided my sadness could only be alleviated by the understanding and company of a woman. Within moments two of the feminine members of the Soviet staff appeared and occupied camp chairs in our little semicircle within the command tent. One of the two was a very pleasant young woman who smiled a good deal of the time, but who nevertheless seemed terribly ill at ease if not distinctly embarrassed. The other, who was quite ugly, gave the impression of being able to kill or maim without remorse. She never smiled, and as I began to lose consciousness from the sustained and rigorous consumption, I had the fleeting impression that she fancied the other woman and certainly not Michael or me.

I drifted off feeling somehow safe—still sad, even bewildered by the previous days and the unreality of the place, but safe and alive. How I came to be in my own sleeping bag in the Soviet staff women's dormitory the next morning I never clearly learned. I awoke to find my arm draped over a figure in a sleeping bag close by, and for a moment I was gripped by the thought I had been kidnapped by the remorseless, ugly one. I noticed then the hair and a trace of beard and that it was Monastyrski with an arm around the pretty one in yet another sleeping bag.

Roskelley, ever the loner when he had to be, escaped Michael's punishing if generous therapy by wandering down the Achik Tash, where he spent the evening and a day with a family of Kirghiz shepherds. John claimed when he returned to have observed from hiding a Soviet military unit moving up the Alai Valley, but the thought of further incident or catastrophe on top of a mega-hangover was too much to face and I begged him not to tell me any more.

CHAPTER EIGHT
▲
Renewed Efforts Above

The American expedition had great momentum, which did not spend itself in the Krylenko avalanche or the death of Gary. Even if we had wanted to and the Soviets had obliged us, we could not have gone home then. We all felt an obligation to continue. Many people had given time and effort and money to make the trip possible. Our real goals had dissolved, but we could at least do Lenin by the standard routes, some could go up—perhaps by a variation on the northeast ridge to the left of the Lipkin ridge and the right of Krylenko face.

We felt we ought to return to Gary if the north face settled enough, and perhaps determine whether we could evacuate his body if enough manpower became available when the climbers returned from the high camps. We all agreed a memorial would be erected to Gary somewhere in the valley. A great rock in the meadow three-quarters of a mile from Base toward the peaks seemed a logical site.

On the morning of July 28, Pete and I called an expedition council. Clouds had again begun to settle on the higher peaks after a day of partial clearing. The new snow covered the upper slopes, and occasional avalanches roared down Krylenko and Peak Nineteen. Mike Yokell's knee was seriously injured from his jump to safety at Crevasse Camp and there was no way he could climb again that summer. He generously volunteered to return to Moscow as quickly as possible to make the necessary arrangements concerning Gary's death—immediate notification of Gary's family by telephone, filing the death certificate, whatever might be necessary. It was not a pleasant or an easy mission, but it was unquestionably the best way the shattering news could be conveyed to the family. The departure from the expedition of Mike, whom we were just coming to know, added to the undefined sense of gloom we all seemed to feel.

We discussed routes, who would go where, equipment —certain items had to be reallocated because of losses in the avalanches; we talked over the reorganization of the teams. Evans remained a center of climbing leadership, and to his team of Carson, Lev, and Stanley he added Marty Hoey and Jed Williamson. Since the return of the teams from Lenin, Marty and Pete Lev had become inseparable, and the ascent of the mountain together took on a new meaning. Schoening's group remained more or less intact, and to Kopczynski and Sarnquist he added Molly Higgins. Both groups would do Lenin via the Razdelny route.

Jock Glidden and Al Steck wanted to at least try a variation of an established route on Lenin. They included Chris Wren, with the thought of attempting one of the buttresses of the northeast ridge. Roskelley and Marts elected to return to Peak Nineteen, possibly accompanied by Jeff Lowe, whose ailing knee might mend in time.

I still felt bad with sore ribs, and my fingertips and toes were numb. Since returning to Base, I had developed stomach and intestinal upset, which ruled out travel at the moment. Pete Schoening had urged me to join his group for old times' sake and that offer was somehow tempting. I decided to wait a day or so and see how I felt, but I knew the disenchantment that had come over me after Gary's death would not pass quickly. There was the beginning outline in my mind of the rationalization that I would be of more value in Base than limping up a mountain that had lost the appeal it had formerly had. In short, though I did not want to admit it, I had no stomach for climbing anymore.

I vaguely hoped I could perform some needed functions of the expedition at Base that would not let the others down. I admired Al Steck all the more as he nursed painful ribs yet moved about camp cheering on the younger climbers to regroup. Peter Lev had made in our group meeting perhaps the most prophetic observation of our journey: "Some summers when things go wrong, they just continue to get worse." That thought probably fueled my rationalization for remaining behind more than anything else.

Members of the group spent the afternoon of July 28 preparing loads, drawing new food supplies from the Soviet commissary, chatting with the Soviet advisers about characteristics of the routes on Lenin. Mike Yokell departed quickly and unceremoniously for Osh and Moscow. Other teams were pushing off for Lenin.

Two German parties were headed up for Camp I on the way to Razdelny Pass, as were a group of Japanese, a large number of Austrians, and the Dutch team. One Scots team headed for the northeast ridge of Lenin. Two teams of French climbers, one with skis for a descent of the north face of Lenin, also struck out toward Razdelny Pass.

Across the stream from the International Camp, a large number of Siberians were preparing to leave for the Lipkin ridge on the north side of Lenin. They were given a cheery send-off by the group of eight Soviet women who would leave the next day for the arduous traverse of Peak Lenin, ascending via the Lipkin ridge, crossing the summit, and descending via the Razdelny route to Camp III and off the mountain by the well-worn route to Camps II and I. No team of women had ever climbed Peak Lenin without the leadership of males, and none had ever made a traverse of the peak. By late afternoon it was snowing again above 18,000 feet.

On July 29, the American teams departed at various times in the morning. There was no evidence of great enthusiasm, but it was obvious everyone was pleased to get clear of the vague feeling of depression that hung over Base Camp.

Another team of Japanese left, headed for the Lipkin ridge, and in the early afternoon the Soviet women departed, singing lovely songs, alternately sad and spirited in tone. We heard their voices like a choir across the great meadow of edelweiss until they had reached the huge rock we had tentatively selected for Gary's memorial.

Doug Scott and his team were extremely concerned about a great amount of valuable camera and expedition equipment they had left cached on the east side of Peak Lenin at the head of the Saukdhara Glacier. They hung back from the other departing groups hoping to negotiate with the Soviets for a truck which could take them south and around to the Saukdhara. From their cache on the east side they would proceed up to Krylenko Pass and then onto the northeast ridge of Lenin, caching their recovered gear on the shoulder. They were also willing to try to recover the most valuable elements of the American cache.

The Soviets were adamant that no one could go around to the Saukdhara. We learned shortly that there may have been a reason for their inflexibility, but as with so many things in the Soviet Union, one could never be sure. The Englishmen took it genially and headed off for a fairly steep, elegant, and, so far as we knew, unclimbed ice ridge leading to the main northeast ridge of Peak Lenin.

By late afternoon, Base Camp was all but empty, and an

eerie peacefulness settled over the Achik Tash Valley. Of the Americans, only four remained: Lowe, Marts, Roskelley, and I. We had requested permission for the three to return to the north face and Camp IV via the northeast ridge to assess the evacuation of Gary's body, and had been informed by Abalakov we would have to wait until the next day. There were very few others around beyond the Soviet support staff for the camp. Two of the Soviet coaches, Kostya and Oleg, remained, and they were preparing to go up to be in a support position at Camp I in the event they were needed anywhere on the mountain. Gippenreiter had remained behind to help with translation for the departing teams and would leave in the morning to join the Siberians on the Lipkin. Viktor and Georg were likewise at Camp III on Razdelny Pass at 20,000 feet. The thought occurred that the Soviets had a serious potential rescue problem with as many climbers of varying degrees of ability as they had on high, storm-swept mountains.

On the morning of July 30 a telegram was delivered:

> Ullin family advised of Gary's death. Request body be evacuated from Peak Nineteen if can be accomplished safely and buried in earth at edge of the glaciers. (Sgd.) Leonard Williams, Counselor, U.S. Embassy, Moscow.

We wondered, What can we say in reply? "No American or Soviet climbers available to effect evacuation at this time." No, that wouldn't do, and besides, it wouldn't be accurate. Even if climbers were available, the conditions were such that we wouldn't try it at that time in any case. We knew, even as we thought about the reply, that it might not be possible to make an attempt at all if it didn't stop snowing at the higher elevations.

The quiet and peacefulness of Base had become ironic. Four remaining Americans, few if any available Soviets, continuing storm, new snow building up to dangerous depths, no real logistical back-up, and we were asked by telegram from Moscow to attempt to recover our companion's body from the 17,000-foot level of an exposed ice face of a high Asiatic mountain. It would have been a major undertaking and not necessarily a feasible one with everyone at hand—now the prospect was just not possible with so little manpower. Still we had to make some kind of effort, if only to assess the evacuation problem itself, or at least to give Gary a more formal burial than we had been able to give him in our flight off the mountain.

When Roskelley saw the telegram, he was halfway out of Base Camp. We quickly pointed out, "We leave when the Soviets agree, John. Not before. They don't want us up there while everyone else is scattered over Lenin in worsening weather."

Monastyrski and Abalakov were, of course, fully aware of the message and its implications, but new emergencies had descended upon them, unbeknownst to us.

"You know about our message from the embassy, Michael?"

"Yes, Robert, we do. It is not an easy situation."

"We must try, Michael!"

"There is something you do not know, something we have learned only now. The five Estonians on Hiebler ridge of the east face of Lenin, who were last seen by your American teammates before the earthquake, have not reported in. There has been no word. We have not heard from them in nine days. A helicopter will come up from Dushanbe, We must find them!"

Since there was basically little we could do at the moment for Gary unless we were to bury him permanently and formally in Camp IV, the crises of the Estonians crowded out consideration of anything else for the moment. We pointed out to Monastyrski and Abalakov that there were four of us, all skilled climbers and expert in mountain rescue, and all very willing to help, especially since there were so few Soviet climbers available.

Monastyrski quickly established the reality of the situation as it applied to the Estonians. He spoke to us as we assembled by his command post next to the radio and communication tent. "The helicopter can only carry one plus the pilot over Krylenko Pass. Krylenko is too high [20,000 feet] for even [a wistful smile] our helicopter. Spotter must know Hiebler ridge. Valodya [a Soviet coach] did the second ascent—so he goes! If we find the Estonians, perhaps the Americans can go with the Soviet rescue team. Otherwise . . ." The assessment and approach seemed very reasonable, but there was a curious feeling in the air. It was as if they knew more, but were going through a necessary ritual.

When we asked Abalakov how they had discovered the Estonians had a problem, he shrugged his shoulders, stared off at Lenin, his bright blue eyes revealing nothing, and said in German, "They are long overdue, there has been no radio message, they have not appeared on this side. It is a hard route. We can only wait."

The helicopter arrived from Osh, the same model that made the drop on Camp IV of Peak Nineteen. Valodya, one of the Masters of Sport assigned to Base Camp, spent some time conferring with Abalakov, Anufrikov, and the natty pilot of the chopper. They looked at maps, but mostly talked intensely, seriously, with heads close together. The pilot and Valodya boarded the craft and were off at 10:00 A.M.

We waited a couple of hours, expecting the aircraft to return with some kind of news. It did not, and we assumed it had gone out via the Saukdhara. By noon we had begun to speculate about what had happened, remembering that Evans's party had seen and photographed a team of five climbers well up on the Hiebler the day before the earthquake.

At lunch Monastyrski reported: "We have no word. The heliplane cannot communicate from the east side of Lenin. They will fly out via the Saukdhara to Dushanbe. A rescue group is on its way up the Saukdhara."

This was the first inkling we had that the Soviets were sufficiently alarmed to mount a major rescue effort. It may also have accounted for the sudden evacuation of the Soviet military mountaineering camp below the Pass of the Travelers. No one saw lorries leave with troops, but there was little left of the camp as we returned from Peak Nineteen, and it became quite conceivable in light of the Estonians' crisis that a rescue effort had been mounted somewhat earlier than anyone knew.

We reiterated our desire to help and said that we could be ready to go at a moment's notice if the Soviets wanted to put us in a truck and haul us around to the terminus of the Saukdhara Glacier. Again the vagueness, the faint sense of evasiveness. They must know something about the helicopter's findings with the fairly sophisticated radio equipment in the communication tent. Surely Osh would be serving as a relay point for communications coming through the military net which undoubtedly covered the entire Pamirs region.

It began to seem that the Soviets had had for some time an inkling of a disaster on the east face and were going through the motions so as not to appear neglectful in the face of a possible disaster involving the Estonians. Why had they waited so long to announce the Estonians' "missing" status? They certainly had known something was up before their announcement in the morning if they had by now a rescue team on the Saukdhara.

We were gaining the impression that the Soviets were ultrasensitive to anything which might bring criticism down on them for mismanagement or neglect in their operation of the large-scale International Camp, yet most of what had taken place thus far fitted in the act-of-God category and no one could reasonably condemn them for bad luck. We wanted to express this to them, but somehow the subtleties of our sentiments got lost in translation.

By evening we were aware of a new, open sense of gloom among our Russian friends. Where they were normally quite self-contained, they now appeared clearly depressed. We asked Vitaly Abalakov what was troubling them. He replied slowly, softly, in precise German, "The helicopter found nothing, no sign. We are afraid they are lost. They were good climbers. It is a shame. The ground party will search to the base of the Hiebler in case some may have got down."

We did not learn until days later that three of the five were swept to their death as the earthquake triggered a massive avalanche of new snow and ice that engulfed the east face like a great wave. The surviving two climbers were badly injured and found by the rescue party at the bottom of the Hiebler. They died after being evacuated to the hospital in Osh.

We were moved by the obvious sadness and dismay of Abalakov, this strong "father of Soviet mountaineering." Over the many years of his distinguished career of climbing in the Pamirs, the Tien Shan, and the Caucasus he had lost most of the fingers of his left hand, part of his right hand, and all the toes on his left foot. He appeared to have a personal involvement with every climber who went out from the Base Camp.

We continued to ponder the telegram from the U.S. Embassy in Moscow and what we could do to fulfill its spirit. With the Estonians beyond any help we could render, we were faced with the problem of recovering or burying Gary and the resistance of the Soviets to our returning to Peak Nineteen. Before the Estonian crisis, Abalakov had indicated his unwillingness to have anyone go on the face. Still, Roskelley was determined to go back, and it was clear in my mind, at least, that he would go whether the Russians agreed or not. That meant some kind of compromise or graceful way out for the Soviets had to be found.

Following the Peak Nineteen episode, the Soviets had required that all teams re-entering the range from Base submit detailed itineraries in writing. We felt that might be the best first step toward indicating we were determined to fulfill our obligation to Gary and the Ullin family.

We submitted to Abalakov the itinerary in memorandum form:

> By cable via the U.S. Embassy in Moscow, the family of Gary Ullin have requested evacuation of Ullin's body from the north face of Peak of the Nineteenth Party Congress. An American team led by John Roskelley and including John Marts and Jeffrey Lowe will attempt to reach Camp IV on the north face via the northeast ridge to ascertain feasibility of recovery of the body. If judged too dangerous or too arduous in light of limited manpower available, the Americans will make a suitable burial of Ullin on the mountain and proceed off the mountain, ascending the remaining ice slope above the camp. Craig will remain in Base to provide liaison and coordination for this operation, as well as any needed coordination and support for the Americans on Peak Lenin.
>
> Robert W. Craig, Deputy Leader
> John Roskelley

In the midst of the Estonian situation, two European visitors arrived at Base. They were Jean Judge and Pierre Bossus, both officials of the Union Internationale des Associations d'Alpinisme. Judge was President of the UIAA and Bossus the Executive Secretary.

They had flown in to observe the International Camp, which was substantially unoccupied on their arrival. They were accompanied by an elderly Russian scientist, a former climbing companion of Abalakov, who spoke English, French, and German fluently.

▲

As we submitted our itinerary to Abalakov, we suggested the new arrival might help out with the translation. We were beginning to realize the vital function of Gippenreiter in the smooth running of the camp; we hoped he was enjoying the simple Spartan pleasure of a high camp on Lenin. But the weather aloft did not necessarily suggest that was likely, as it had begun to storm all the way down to Base, with rain, thunder, lightning, and new snow down as low as 15,000 feet.

After dinner and during the downpour, the principal diversion from boredom was provided by the concertina playing of one of the Russian camp roustabouts and the nightly movies in the cinema tent. The music, by a round-faced Muscovite also named Valody, ran the range from well-known folk songs and Red Army ballads to a few Broadway hits, and reached moments of real poignancy when he played and sang "Stenka Razin." Three Russian movies rotated night after night, largely for our audience of Kirghiz herdsmen, who spent most of their days out in the vast, lonely ranges of the Pamirs and who journeyed in by horse and truck from all over the grasslands leading to the Lenin massif. The camp and the movies must have seemed like an oasis to these authentic refugees from another age.

One film told the story of a group of attractive Polish mountain partisans and their brave but hopeless struggle against the Nazis. It was not unlike watching a certain kind of western—the audience cheered loudly for the Poles and jeered and booed the Nazis. For an ideological film, the climbing and skiing scenes were surprisingly good. One of the Russian films was an adaptation of the Italian film *The Red Tent,* and for some reason that was hard to define at the moment, that tragic epic about an exploratory expedition of Italians who were trying to be the first to gain the

North Pole began to have a strange congruence with what was taking shape as the Pamirs summer.

The third Soviet-produced film was a lugubrious story of a Russian cross-country ski racer widowed by World War II who, by dint of great sacrifice, kept her daughter in the academy of music, and ultimately married the only conceivable and decent man who could replace her fallen hero husband. I remember thinking it was probably better fare under the circumstances than *Midnight Cowboy.*

The Kirghiz who came in from remote corners of the northern Pamirs were probably not unlike American Indians in the 1930s and '40s coming in from the reservations in Wyoming or Montana to the movie houses of Sheridan or Livingston or Buffalo, strangers in their own land, fascinated by a new technology.

▲

The next morning, July 31, sixteen days after we had arrived in the Achik Tash Valley, we met Monastyrski and Abalakov in the mess tent. They were entertaining the two Swiss UIAA visitors. The atmosphere was cordial, but we sensed a certain reserve, indeed embarrassment, from the two Soviets in whom we had come to develop a deep sense of trust. We knew they did not want us to go to Peak Nineteen. We did not know the precise reasons, but we knew the word was out: "Curb danger, risk, and embarrassment to the visitors." Not an entirely unreasonable way of looking at things if one had 160 visitors climbing dangerous high mountains in one of the more sensitive frontiers in the world, and six of them already dead.

By midmorning we felt we had to know. Time was running out. Roskelley was explosive; he would go whether permission was granted or not. We could not, in good conscience, try to hold Marts, Lowe, and Roskelley unless the Russians established an adequate reason for our not at least attempting to evacuate Gary's body. We went to Monastyr-

177

ski's command tent. "You are going to deny us permission to evacuate Gary. We can feel it!"

"I did not—we did not say anything like 'deny.' It is a matter of timing. Perhaps later. Now it is very dangerous. You are our guests. Maybe six climbers dead. Others are climbing Lenin; the storm continues. What would you do if you were in our place?" He was not far from a very basic truth. We would have done very much the same thing under the circumstances. Perhaps we would have been even tougher, less accommodating.

We said, "Michael, we understand and sympathize with your situation, but you of all people should know that we have a moral obligation to make an effort to recover Gary's body if that is what the parents want."

"You are like brothers. You must trust me. We do not have enough reserves to help anyone who is in trouble. If they go and something happens, what do we say when Moscow asks why the Americans went back to the scene of a disaster? No. It is a bad summer; we cannot have any more trouble. Please try to understand."

The plea to back off from our plan was so simple, so straightforward, so understandable; yet we had an honor-bound request from a dead friend's family. Gary's father was a retired guide—surely he knew the limits and would understand if we finally had to give up the recovery; but we had to try. We drafted a new message to Leonard Williams at the U.S. Embassy in Moscow:

> American team wishes to fulfill parents' request recover Ullin's body but Soviet authorities gravely worried conditions too dangerous for evacuation north face Peak Nineteen. May not be able attempt reach body for final formal burial. Regards.

The message never reached the communication tent. We had presented the cable to Misha, the French- and English-speaking Russian meteorologist, a courtly, elderly man who seemed continually astonished by the weather that summer, and had asked that he translate it into Russian for transmission. An hour or so later Abalakov sent a messenger asking us to come to his tent, which we did immediately. Speaking in German, he said, "I cannot authorize the American team's going back to Peak Nineteen. What can three of you do? It has continued to snow every day since you returned. The mountains are all waiting to fall. You are my responsibility. Please do not send the message. Wait at least until conditions change. Then we will go with you."

We argued back and forth on the matter for almost another day before we presented Abalakov with a face-saving compromise in the form of a statement that we hoped would allow us to do the appropriate thing for Gary's family and protect Abalakov and Monastyrski from excessive responsibility.

We finally said, "We have to admit that if we were in Mr. Abalakov's position, we would take the same position. They must consider the good of all the climbers. On the other hand, we are caught with our own obligations. We would like to propose a proposition: we will put in writing a statement holding harmless all Soviet authorities of the International Climbing Camp for the actions of the American team which will endeavor to reach and bury the body of Jon Gary Ullin. We accept the sound view that the conditions for this effort are far from adequate, but we know, too, that time is rapidly running out and we must at least be able to report to the family that we tried. Otherwise, we must report that we were not permitted to try."

Suddenly the conflict was over. Michael winked at us; Abalakov nodded, looking wistful, smiling faintly. Yes, that would be acceptable. They would like the statement to be very explicit.

The statement we had agreed to draft was delivered to Abalakov and Monastyrski that night:

STORM AND SORROW IN THE HIGH PAMIRS

> The American Pamirs Expedition, having been requested by the parents of Jon Gary Ullin to recover or at least permanently bury the body of their son *in situ*, wish to state that they are undertaking the effort against the better judgment of their Russian hosts. The American group accepts full responsibility in undertaking to fulfill this cabled request . . .

Marts, Lowe, and Roskelley were off in midmorning of August 1. Monastyrski kindly provided a truck to take them up to the glacier edge. I rode with them. Roskelley still did not understand what had happened, but they were on their way. The upper part of Nineteen was again going under storm as they descended the long, steep slope toward the moraine of the North Face Glacier.

Shortly after Lowe, Marts, and Roskelley had left, we received another message from Mr. Williams at the U.S. Embassy in Moscow:

> Ullin family recognize danger involved evacuation Gary's body north face. Appreciate burial on mountain and memorial in meadow below. Regards. Leonard Williams.

We replied:

> Message of 8/1 received and understood. Recovery effort is canceled. Climbing party enroute prepare if possible final resting place. Letters to Ullin family follow.

CHAPTER NINE
▲
Heavy Traffic in Bad Weather

Base Camp was almost completely empty by the afternoon. Even Monastyrski had left for a day and a half's visit to Osh. There had been so much rain and snow in the area that the ground had become sodden. Shepherds had moved large herds of sheep and goats onto the lower, heavily grassed slopes of Peak Petrovski rising above Base and there was an almost constant tinkling of bells on the lead animals, the periodic barking of the fierce dogs tending the flocks, and the occasional high-pitched, mournful-sounding cry of one neighboring young shepherd to another.

Misha, the multilingual Soviet interpreter, was usually available and always helpful in providing translation at the communication tent, and in that way I was able to gain some daily sense of the status of the Americans and many others on Peak Lenin.

By the afternoon of August 2, Schoening's group had arrived at a crowded Camp III at about 6,000 meters (19,685 feet). In the space of a few yards, in random ranks, some in the lee of an overhanging crevasse, were the tents of the Scots, Austrians, Japanese, Dutch, Swiss, Germans, and Americans. Camp III at Razdelny Pass was far more cosmopolitan than Base because of the diversity of the tents' design and color; but it was also a scene of desolate mess. There was garbage and human waste everywhere.

There had been no word from Jock Glidden, Al Steck, and Chris Wren since their departure July 29, but the radio operator noted that the Siberians had reported seeing the Americans midway on the Lipkin ridge on the morning of August 2. The English and three of the Scots had completed a good line on the northeast buttress on Lenin and were well up the main northeast ridge. The Soviet women had reported in two-thirds of the way up the Lipkin, going strong and in fine spirits.

Almost all parties reporting expressed concern about the uncertainty of the weather and asked Base for the latest meteorological data. The available weather information was equivocal—the Soviet Meteorological Center at Osh was forecasting on August 2: "Unsettled conditions over the Pamirs, with no definite signs of frontal formation." They were also not forecasting any prospect of general clearing, and everyone was painfully aware of the fact that it had snowed at the upper elevations virtually every day since July 15. Almost three weeks of continuous if sometimes incipient storm, and now over 75 climbers were converging from several directions on the 23,406-foot summit of Lenin.

Lowe, Marts, and Roskelley reached the northeast ridge of Peak Nineteen late in the afternoon of August 1 and set up camp as it began to rain. They were in the saddle below the point where we had been met by the three French climbers (Bernard, François, and Yves), John Evans, and Fred Stanley. They had gone up very rapidly, and Marts arrived at the campsite at 14,000 feet knowing he would have to return to Base. He simply never recovered from the infection that had plagued him ever since Seattle.

The next morning, as Marts descended to Base, John and Jeff continued on to the site of Camp IV. As they climbed, they assessed the possibility of evacuating Gary's body, and long before they arrived at the camp it was apparent that two and a half weeks of continuous snow made the route far too hazardous, not to mention too deep in places to work in. The avalanche hazard was, if anything, worse than when we had been there. They reached the camp by midafternoon and immediately set about locating Gary's body. They found Gary as we had left him before, dug out a larger shelf, wrapped his body in a larger American flag, and observed a few respectful moments. When they had covered the body, they reset the crossed Russian skis over the grave.

As they buried him for the last time, they both realized they had one last gesture to make on behalf of Gary—to finish the route we had all begun on Nineteen, direct up the ice face above the camp. Roskelley writes:

> After we had buried Gary, we vowed to go for the summit in his memory. We felt it was at least as safe as the slope we had crossed from the northeast ridge. We worked on a snow cave in the same serac we used before. It became a palace with standing room, kitchen shelves and sleeping shelves in no time. We spent an eerie night, myself feeling the presence of a third party.
>
> 3:30 a.m. and a quick meal. I led up in deep snow and crossed the bergschrund onto the main face. We donned crampons and Jeff led off, going for three leads, as we didn't stop to belay. The face did not present much difficulty for 2,000 feet, so we changed leads every three rope lengths. As we approached the upper rock bands, the snow became loose, unconsolidated and deep. The slope steepened considerably. Jeff, fighting for every inch, led over iced rock and protectionless deep spindrift. Swimming was the order of the day.
>
> My lead did the same, but ended at the feel of consolidated snow. Jeff took off on solid ground until he reached

the last rock band. Putting in a hope and a prayer for hardware, he brought me to the tiny stance he called "home." The last lead was touchy. I moved left gaining height on small, icy holds, wondering why there never is any protection on the top lead of good climbs. We arrived on the summit about the same time as clouds, snow and lightning.

What had begun as one of the most challenging problems of the summer ended in a funeral and in a fine ascent.

▲

John Marts had arrived back the previous afternoon. We had observed the completion of the climb of Peak Nineteen's north face by Jeff and John on August 3, between breaks in the clouds, and there was a profound sense of relief in seeing them arrive safely on top.

We had feared that the snow on the final part of the face might release at any moment, but they had put in an excellent, perfectly direct line, completing their effort as the storm began anew. We approached Abalakov's tent and informed the old man that John and Jeff had gotten up safely. He smiled thinly, eyes crinkling, and said, "That is good." He should have been greatly relieved but was clearly worried, and we suspected he was still shaken about the loss of the Estonians. What he was really concerned about was the unimproving weather and the almost unheard of numbers of climbers on a 23,406-foot mountain.

We heard on the radio from Razdelny that Higgins, Kopczynski, Sarnquist, and Schoening had gone straight through to Camp III on August 2 and climbed Lenin on the third. Molly Higgins was the first American to reach the summit of the peak. The French from Grenoble reached the summit also, as did the Parisians. Three of the latter descended the north side of Lenin on skis and reported that the skiing was not particularly worth the effort. Doug Scott, Tut Braithwaite, Paul Nunn, and Guy Lee reached the summit via Lipkin, greeting the Soviet women as they passed their camp. The weather appeared to be worsening at the higher levels, but Evans's team would go for the summit on the fourth. Schoening's group returned from the summit to Camp III on the third.

John Evans's group got off early for the summit of Lenin on the morning of August 4, too early to be aware that Vitaly Abalakov had radioed to Georg and Viktor, the two Soviet coaches in charge of Camp III at Razdelny Pass, announcing that Osh was now forecasting a storm of major proportions that was expected to last for the next several days. He recommended that everyone descend immediately. It was not a direct order, but it was put so strongly that no one could have any doubts about the potential seriousness of the situation. The message was received not only at Razdelny, but also, we learned later, by the Soviet women, the Japanese, and the Siberians on the Lipkin.

Evans, Bruce Carson, Marty Hoey, Peter Lev, and Jed Williamson went up in very marginal conditions which turned into a whiteout as they reached the summit. Jed was not feeling well part way up and returned to Camp III. As Evans and the others returned to Razdelny, he, Stanley, and Carson decided to continue on to Camp II. Peter Lev and Marty Hoey agreed to stay at III in a support position for another day while Jed made a second bid for the summit.

Also on August 4, Allen North, the Scottish doctor, arrived alone on top via the northeast ridge after a solo bivouac. As he climbed down, he encountered the Soviet women moving up slowly but in high spirits. Farther down, near the top of the Lipkin, Allen encountered Glidden, Steck, and Wren in the camp and stopped for a welcome cup of tea.

August 5 dawned relatively clear and calm in Camp III. Several climbers who had not made the summit, in addition to Jed Williamson, decided to chance the weather,

185

regardless of the dire warnings, and make one more try before abandoning the mountain. Among these were a Japanese group who in one of the summer's rare moments of humor had dubbed themselves the "Escargots." Three Scottish climbers—Ronnie Richards, Ian Fulton, and Graham Tiso—also set out on the fifth. The International "Ladies"—a group composed of Heidi Ludi; Eva Eissenschmidt; the Bavarian model Anya; and Arlene Blum, an American biochemist originally in the Soviet Union for a scientific meeting, who joined the women in Moscow—all left a bit later, intending to establish a higher camp and go up on August 6.

Jed left at about 7:00 A.M., hoping to catch up with the Japanese and proceed to the summit with them. He passed the ladies' group by midmorning and, climbing on alone, arrived on the summit plateau about noon as ominous storm clouds were building in the southwest. He had set 2:30 P.M. as his safe turn-back time.

As he reached 22,800 feet, he noted it was close to 2:30 P.M. The Japanese were some 50 yards ahead. He called to them, suggesting they all turn back. They replied they were determined to go on despite the threatening weather.

As Jed noted, "Not being one for conversation in such circumstances I turned around and went down." Jed turned back short of the summit, having made the prudent decision that going on in the face of worsening weather and a late hour could be disastrous.

Descending toward Camp III, Jed came across three of the International Women at about 21,500 feet. Blum had apparently decided to go down, leaving the two Swiss, Heidi and Eva, and the Bavarian Anya. Heidi was in search of a tent platform on the long sloping neve field, and below her, off to one side, perched on the rock, Anya and Eva sat, back to back, chattering and seemingly in good spirits. Their plan was to bivouac and go for the summit the next day. Jed said something about the threatening storm and Abalakov's warning and continued down.

A few hundred feet below the International "Ladies," Jed came upon Arlene Blum, seemingly lost and searching for the way down to Camp III. Jed offered to help find the way down. Strong winds and blowing snow hit then, buffeting them in several directions, and they had to fight their way down against the gusts and rapidly drifting snows in the lee of the west ridge to Camp III. As they descended in the increasing gale, which Jed had sensed to be the beginning of the forecasted major storm, they knew everyone above would soon be in serious trouble. The International Women did not even have a tent erected, and they would be hard put to get one up now that the storm had set in. Jed and Arlene themselves were in a serious situation, but at least they were headed down and toward the security of Camp III.

Arlene was very tired and, as Jed thought, disoriented —a common enough disability at that altitude; she continually wanted to sit down as the storm began in earnest. It was snowing harder, and the winds were above 60 miles an hour. Jed refused to stop, forced the pace with harangues and insults, and they tumbled into Camp III thoroughly chilled and at the edge of their reserves of strength.

Around 4:30 P.M., the Japanese party and the team of Scots reached the summit of Lenin. The weather was rapidly worsening, but the Scots took time to photograph the great aluminum bust of Nikolai Lenin with a bottle of Glenlivet that they pressed to his lips.

As they prepared to descend, another series of ropes appeared on the summit from the opposite direction of the northeast and Lipkin ridges. It was the Soviet women's team, two ropes of four each, cheerful but very tired, having carried full loads to the summit and close to achieving the first all-female traverse of the peak. They planned to go down the west side to Camp III at Razdelny Pass, and on to Camps II and I and home to Base.

Ronnie Richards, who spoke Russian fairly fluently, urged the women to descend quickly from the summit, as the large storm that had been predicted was already being felt with heavily gusting winds and blowing snow.

The ladies were adamant that they would not descend, but pitch camp on the summit of Peak Lenin. Elvira Shataeyeva, the leader, told Richards, "We are strong. We are Soviet women. It is late and we are tired. We will camp here and go down to Razdelny tomorrow." The Scots descended into the storm as the Soviet women began pitching their tents.

Shortly after Jed and Arlene had been settled in Marty and Peter's tent, Jed explained the desperate situation he suspected developing 1,500 feet above. The storm continued to build, and communication between other parts of the camp was well nigh impossible, but Pete felt an urgent need to assemble a rescue team to make an effort in the morning. There was no possibility of setting out in the storm at the moment. They could only hope the International Women could hold out through the night. Nearby, two of the French climbers from Grenoble were camped, resting from their climb of the day before. François Valla and Michel Vincent were two of the strongest members of the Grenoble University mountaineering team, and François, like Peter Lev an avalanche researcher, had assisted the Americans on Peak Nineteen. Pete crawled into their tent and described the situation confronting the International Women. They agreed to move out early in the morning, enlisting whatever aid they could find in the camp.

One wonders what might have happened had it not been for the fortuitous combination of Peter; the two Frenchmen; the German, Sepp Schwankener; and the two Netherlanders, Hans and Louie. François Valla later reported that the two Soviet coaches seemed unable to comprehend the seriousness of the situation above, nor did they see the need to prepare a rescue or even a reconnaissance of the upper mountain to determine the condition of the International Women. Indeed, there were not only the three women bivouacking high above Camp III in the storm, but the three Japanese and a Swiss climber as well. They were not yet aware of what was taking place on the summit of Lenin where the eight Soviet women had established camp.

Peter described the rescue of the International Women in his accident report to the Soviet authorities:

> Jed Williamson's report on August 5th that the three Swiss girls planned to bivouac above Camp III on Peak Lenin caused concern among those 17 or so people from different nations camped at Camp III. That late afternoon and through the night a storm raged which appeared very serious to me. We received about a foot of new snow at Camp III, accompanied by wind.
>
> The morning of August 6th arrived with the storm in greater force. High winds were beginning to affect the sheltered side of Camp III. There was no doubt that we would have to look for the Swiss girls as we were deeply concerned for their safety. When I say "we," I believe this includes all the people at Camp III. However, I was only in close communication with the other two Americans, Marty Hoey and Jed Williamson, and the two French climbers, François Valla and Michel Vincent.
>
> François and Michel and I were the ones to go because we were the strongest and most experienced climbers in Camp III. We had also rested the previous day, the day J. Williamson made his summit attempt. Michel carried a pack with a tent, drinks and first aid supplies. Two Dutch and one West German (by the name of Sepp Schwankener, later to play an important, helpful part) accompanied us. A couple of hundred feet above Camp III these three turned back. The winds were up to 70+ mph, blizzard and very cold.
>
> François, Michel and I had ascended somewhat more than halfway the big step above Camp III when we met Anya descending alone. She repeated over and over that Eva kept falling down when we asked her about the other two girls.

She also said that she had left them twenty minutes before. This indicated to me that the girls were on the flat above the first step. Michel descended with Anya to assure her safe return to Camp III. François took the sack, and he and I proceeded up the ridge.

The blizzard seemed even more fierce as François and I topped out on the flat above the big step. We stopped momentarily while I took a compass reading so that we could find our way back to this spot. That completed, I turned around to start walking along the flat. A short distance away was a rucksack. I ran up to it, and then saw to the northeast about 100 feet away two figures huddled in the blizzard, amongst the exposed rocks. I ran over first, François right behind me. One girl, Eva, was lying down, groaning and moving about in a slow rolling manner. Her hands were exposed, no hat. The other girl, Heidi, was sitting and holding a tangled rope by which she held Eva on a tight hand-held belay. Heidi was very cold and very white in the face, but still able to communicate and function. Eva could not communicate and was delirious. François tried to administer some drink to Eva, it was impossible.

The gusts were now up to 80 mph. There was no place to escape from the wind. We could not erect the tent. Our only choice seemed to be to try to get Eva down. With considerable difficulty, François and I slid Eva into the tent. We also put my cagoule on Eva. We tied Eva into the tent with the rope and prepared to belay her down. With Heidi we rigged a waist sling and carabiner and clipped her onto the rope.

François and I were obliged to begin our belay-lower from the spot where we had found Eva as we could not carry her back to the true ridge crest. Thus the lowering procedure took us out onto the north-facing aspect of the main ridge crest. Our rope was approximately 80 feet long, and we made at least ten lowers. At first the slope was very hard due to the snow having been blown away by the wind. I belayed with an ice axe while François guided Eva and tried to always pull her back to the ridge crest. We were always making a diagonal lower. Frequently François would check Eva.

Then we came into an area of even deeper snow. At this

point, out of the storm appeared Sepp Schwankener, a Bavarian, alone. Now with Sepp's help we were able to further belay and pull Eva through the deep snow. But now, finally, we were getting so far from the ridge crest and out onto the north face that we just could not pull her through the deep snow anymore, so we stopped. We decided that François would go down to Camp III, now close, for help and take Heidi with him. We were concerned that Eva was near death.

Eva was not moving anymore. Sepp began to give her artificial respiration and continued for some time, about 20 minutes. Then I gave her artificial respiration for a while. Then Sepp again. Then we sat there because Eva was dead.

I felt that the snow conditions on the slope that we were on were such that a dangerous slab was developing. Avalanche danger was becoming imminent. Nobody was coming from below. As we had been doing all the way down, we shouted and blew our whistles some more.

Then we covered Eva's body better with the cagoule, and Sepp secured the rope to one of his ski poles which he planted in the snow, and we traversed off the slope. A couple hundred feet down the ridge we met Jed Williamson and several others ascending. We said there was no need, and we all descended to Camp III.

CHAPTER TEN
▲
Storm and Sorrow

In Base, on August 4, we were almost ankle deep in mud after another night of snow and rain. Climbers came down off Peak Lenin in a steady stream. Roskelley and Lowe had returned from Nineteen; Schoening, Higgins, Kopczynski, and Sarnquist from Lenin; and the American sector of Base came back to life again. Austrians, Swiss, English, Russians, and Bavarians all came in as afternoon clouds again enveloped the range.

Jeff and John rapidly crossed the meadow into Base; and while they were not jubilant at having completed the best route of the season, there was the quiet sense of satisfaction at having accomplished a worthwhile task. Peak Nineteen had been a challenge, a drama, a tragedy; and now what had begun with such high spirits and sunlight was completed quietly and in storm. There was no triumph, only a grave on the mountain and two friends safely returned.

With Pete Schoening back, we tried to take stock of the various Americans. Everyone seemed okay at Camp II and ought to be back in Base on August 5. We had not heard a thing from Jock Glidden, Al Steck, and Chris Wren since they left Base Camp. Then there was the report of the Siberians having sighted the Americans on the Lipkin on the second, but the latest long-range weather report had come in forecasting an extremely dangerous new storm. If they were not transmitting, we wondered if they could be receiving. There was some reassurance for their safety in the many years of big-mountain experience of Steck and Glidden; but the big Pamirs storm, with hard snowfall already hitting Base, was the beginning of real anxiety for all of us.

It snowed moderately the night of the fourth; still the storm did not materialize, and we awoke with hopes that conditions would hold until everyone was in a safe position. The morning report of the Soviet coaches at Camp III on the fifth indicated relatively calm conditions with little wind and partly cloudy skies. It had not snowed any appreciable amount the night before.

What was disturbing about their transmission, especially to Abalakov and the other Soviet officials, was the report that climbers were still setting off for the summit in spite of the warnings from Base. Abalakov decided to send up several of the Soviet coaches to be in position to render assistance for those climbers on the Lipkin and Razdelny routes, should they need it on their way down the mountain. Boris and Valodya were already in Camp I and he would immediately dispatch Kostya and Oleg. They would go as high as they could, perhaps to the ice cave camp on the Lipkin.

Abalakov, Gippenreiter, and Monastyrski were in a corner of the mess tent in midafternoon when Pete, John Evans, and I approached them. We said we would like to help if support was needed. Abalakov noted it was too soon, that not enough was known about what was happening on the upper mountain. Monastyrski conveyed a sense of deep concern. By nature he was cheerful, and often humorous, even while functioning in a low-key businesslike manner. He was obviously worried and tense and appeared to be smoking one cigarette after the other. Gippenreiter, normally outgoing and urbane, looked thoroughly exhausted and was distinctly concerned. He had been high on the Lipkin with the Siberians and the Scots. He had had a meal with the Soviet women. Having climbed Lenin four times, he had decided to descend alone after reaching the point where the Lipkin joined the northeast ridge at about 22,000 feet. He said the conditions were as bad as he had ever seen on Peak Lenin. Abalakov was more impassive than ever.

Late in the afternoon of the fifth the storm, which we observed lashing the upper levels of Peak Lenin and the other peaks of the Pamirs within our view, moved down into the Achik Tash Valley. It began again to snow heavily, the wind rose, and we knew the major storm forecast by Osh had arrived. To make things even more ominous, the Soviet Meteorological Service was forecasting "winds of hurricane force." At about 5:00 P.M., Allen North came down off the Lipkin and reported the three Americans were camped solid at about 21,000 feet and planning to go for the summit with the first good weather.

At about 7:00 P.M., we were called to the communication tent and informed by Abalakov and Monastyrski that the Soviet women had indeed reported from the summit of Lenin that they were going to camp on top and that they were having trouble getting their tents up in the storm. It was never clear how many they were able to pitch, though it seemed they had started with three. Abalakov again had ordered them to descend immediately in the morning, returning down the Lipkin, as that was the route they knew. It was almost a 4,000-foot descent to Camp III at Razdelny Pass with virtually no protection in between. By contrast, to the Lipkin ridge from the summit and some sort of lee shelter it was a 1,000–1,500-foot descent. In the back of his mind he hoped, too, that the women might encounter the Japanese or Americans holding out in the storm on the Lipkin. Abalakov suggested further that, as the storm was out of the southwest, they would gain some benefit from the lee of the northeasterly trending Lipkin ridge.

Equally ominous was Monastryski's report that Viktor and Georg had called in a few minutes earlier with the news that it appeared the International Women were in trouble and that a rescue group was being formed at Raz- delny to give assistance in the morning. They reported violent winds, heavy snow, and rapidly falling tempera- tures. Michael also noted that a large group of Siberian and Polish climbers was descending the Lipkin and northeast ridges but was too far below to be of possible assistance to the Soviet women.

The atmosphere in the mess tent that evening was ex- tremely subdued. Over forty people were at 20,000 feet or above, eight of them at 23,400 feet in a great storm that had not even reached its peak. Still, there was no certain indi- cation that anything had gone wrong. The movies went on as scheduled, but attendance was light; and as we returned to our tents, it was snowing hard.

There were five inches of snow on the ground when we got up early the morning of August 6. The sun came out and took some of the chill from the air, and we had the impression that things might be improving. But a look to- ward Peak Lenin was not reassuring: clouds enveloped the whole mountain down to the base, and where a rent oc- curred to reveal layer upon layer of clouds well above 30,000 feet, one could estimate that the winds aloft had to be enormous. This was soon confirmed.

At 8:00 A.M., Viktor and Georg reported from Camp III that the night had been desperate: two tents had been blown apart and the occupants forced to double up with others nearby. The three International Women, Heidi,

Eva, and Anya, were still 1,500 feet or so above Camp III in God knows what shape. There had been over a foot of snow, and the wind was blowing 70 to 80 miles per hour. A rescue team of Peter Lev, François Valla, Michel Vincent, Sepp Schwankener, Hans Bruntjes, and another Netherlander named Louie had left to render assistance in getting them back to the relative safety of Camp III. Three Japanese and a Swiss man were also unaccounted for, and the two Soviet coaches could only hope they managed to bivouac safely.

The Soviet women reported in rather matter-of-factly with a strong signal from their position on the summit of Lenin. They had had a bad night. The wind had destroyed two of their tents in the night. They were now four in each of the two remaining military tents. One of the girls who had been in a collapsed tent was feeling poorly.

The tents had no zipper closures, but rather a double flap system of folds which were secured along the seams by wooden toggles passed through string eyelets attached to the flaps. This closure system hardly kept out the storm in the same kind of tents which were provided for us at Base, and a number of us were dumbfounded when we learned that this equipment was what the Soviet women were depending on. Even more depressing was the knowledge that the four poles providing the A-frame suspension at either end of the two-man tents were made of wood, and at least three or four of these poles had broken in various instances in Base Camp, most not involving heavy winds, but snow loads of a mere few inches. We made no mention of our feeling about the tents to the Soviet officials, but fervently hoped the women could somehow dig snow caves.

Shataeyeva did not specify how or to what degree her teammate was sick. She was apparently one of the two youngest. Michael Monastyrski and Eugene Gippenreiter translated for us alternately as Abalakov, speaking directly to Elvira, the leader, and to each of the women as team-mates, ordered an immediate descent to the shelter of the Lipkin. As they verified their understanding, the roaring wind periodically obliterated their voices. Abalakov, speaking slowly, told the women they had to get down the mountain far enough to find snow suitable for snow caves. He repeated that snow caves and some lee shelter out of the wind were absolutely essential. Again, they must go down the Lipkin immediately. He did not say it directly, but it was implied that if the sick girl could not move and they could not achieve adequate shelter, they must leave her for the good of the group as a whole. He said this softly but he was adamant that they descend. He exacted a prom-ise from Shataeyeva that they would do so.

As we walked back to the American tents, Pete said, "We've got to do something! We've got to persuade them to bring helicopters. There must be some way. They're all going to die up there! Jock, Allen, Chris—they're up there too. At least let's put a rescue or support team together." We agreed to talk to the Russians, the English, and the French and see what could be arranged.

At about 3:00 P.M. on August 6, Viktor called Base from Camp III saying Eva Eissenschmidt had died while being evacuated to Camp III. The other two women had been returned safely, but frostbitten. He noted there was other frostbite among the climbers in the camp and that supplies of fuel and food in the camp were dangerously low. The three Japanese and the Swiss had survived their bivouac and returned to Camp III as the rescue of Eva proceeded. When Abalakov asked Viktor whether they could descend in the storm, he said Peter Lev, the American avalanche specialist, had stated emphatically that snow conditions were just too dangerous for a descent at that time. He noted that he, Georg, and François Valla, another avalanche ex-pert, tended to agree, but he felt they would be in equally grave danger if they remained too long at III.

At 5:00 P.M., the Soviet women called Base from just below the summit of Lenin on the short, steep snow and ice slope leading northeasterly down to the Lipkin. One of the women had died, apparently while assisting the others down. It sounded as if she had frozen to death while belaying the others down to a bivouac position. The girl who had been reported sick was worse and another ill. Under the circumstances of storm and extreme cold and 23,000 feet, being "ill" could only mean that two more were, in fact, dying.

Shataeyeva said they were trying to pitch tents on the steep ridge. Abalakov tried to be stern as he questioned why they had not dug snow caves, but he visibly sagged and seemed more desolate than ever as Elvira replied they had tried but the snow was too hard and that they were very cold and rapidly weakening.

Abalakov then said they must continue to climb down, there was nothing they could do for the sick—they would all die if they tried to remain in that spot. Shataeyeva replied with some detachment that she understood, that they would continue to try, and that they hoped to get farther down the next morning. The Russian woman translating in English next to us said tearfully, "It is like a dream; she doesn't seem to realize what is happening to them."

As Elvira ended her transmission on a note of what seemed deep sadness and resignation, if not of a dangerous kind of vagueness, the steady moan of the raging storm could be clearly heard above her voice; and as it was snowing again at Base, one could only guess at the temperature at 23,000 feet, some 12,000 feet above us. At the adiabatic cooling rate of five or six degrees per 1,000 feet, it was probably somewhere between 60 and 70 degrees below freezing—30 to 40 degrees below zero Fahrenheit. If one added the velocity of the wind, probably well over 70 miles per hour, the prospect of the women's surviving the night seemed very slight.

A crowd of climbers from every national group in Base Camp milled around the communication tent in the falling snow and gloom. The final realization that a disaster of overwhelming proportions was in the making—a disaster that very conceivably might involve everyone on the upper slopes of Lenin—was painfully evident.

Pete and I talked with the British and French about mounting some kind of rescue or assistance effort. The response from Doug Scott and Benoit Renard had been immediate and affirmative. If the Soviets would agree, we would add four English, four French, and four Americans to their coaches at the bottom of the Lipkin and Razdelny routes. We would recommend bringing up helicopters at the earliest moment—tomorrow, the seventh (but requesting them immediately)—if possible to attempt an airdrop to the women. An airdrop or any use of helicopters assumed a lessening of the storm, but experience had indicated that it took at least a day to move machines into position in the Achik Tash Valley.

We would also recommend that the Soviets strongly urge the evacuation of Camp III, despite the known avalanche hazard, in light of the strong possibility that its inhabitants, like the Soviet women, might soon experience the beginnings of hypothermia and reduced function.

We approached our three Russian friends after dinner. We outlined the situation as we saw it and told them of the willingness, indeed the eagerness and necessity, of a group of top climbers making an effort to assist the others. At first there was reluctance, even slight annoyance, and Michael said, "We feel this is our problem. We appreciate your spirit, but we will do everything that can be done."

I replied, "Michael, we understand you are doing everything you can, but it is not enough. You have a rescue operation under way on the Saukdhara Glacier, your coaches are thinly scattered on Peak Lenin, and now there is a real question about the safety of over forty people

199

distributed all over the mountain, a good many of them in places we're not even sure of. We have twelve or so international-class climbers, including a doctor, who are willing to go up to help. They may not succeed, but we must at least try. You must know we are your friends—we will do nothing to embarrass you."

Monastyrski looked at us, eyes slightly brimming, and said, "I know, we have already become better friends. I will discuss this with Evgeny and Vitaly." The three were in session for over an hour. They called us back to the command post at about 7:30 P.M.

Abalakov was, as we had expected, uneasy about the thought of any further exposure of foreign climbers to the hazards of the full storm that was now enveloping the Pamirs, yet he recognized the soundness of our logic. There was no denying that Soviet personnel were stretched too thin. Too many things had happened; even the safety-conscious Soviets could not have predicted so many misfortunes.

Abalakov affirmed that he knew the British, French, and Americans would do nothing to embarrass or distort the situation. Still, what really could be done? The "girls" were 12,000 feet above Base Camp.

Gippenreiter and Monastyrski, knowing as did Abalakov that the chances were very slim for the Russian women, felt there was a chance to render real assistance to those at Camp III and perhaps the Americans, Japanese, and Siberians on the Lipkin. They quietly urged the joint effort. Abalakov, for whom we had by now developed real affection in addition to respect, looked at us sternly and sympathetically and finally said in German, "Yes, we must, in the last analysis, try to do something."

Vitaly Abalakov had staked his reputation and prestige on the enterprise of an all-women's traverse of Peak Lenin. There had been considerable resistance to Abalakov's progressiveness in certain circles of the Soviet Federation of

Mountaineering. Although the general lot of women in the Soviet Union is touted by the authorities as a kind of co-equal existence in all walks of life, and clearly Soviet women in athletics have been a formidable force in international competition, there had been a reluctance in the area of mountaineering to allow female teams to operate on their own in the highest mountains.

We outlined our thoughts regarding the form we thought the rescue group ought to take: the English would be Tut Braithwaite, Guy Lee, Paul Nunn, and Doug Scott; the French would send Bernard Germain, Yves Morin, Benoit Renard, and Michel Revard; and the Americans would include John Evans, Jeff Lowe, John Roskelley, and Frank Sarnquist.

The three Soviet leaders agreed they should go up in the morning and join forces with Kostya, Boris, Oleg, and Valodya. They had already requested helicopter assistance from Dushanbe and from Osh. There was no way to estimate when the planes could reach the Achik Tash. So far as the evacuation of Camp III was concerned, they agreed the Soviet coaches should be urged to descend, but that Peter Lev's concerns about avalanche hazard should be taken most seriously. In any event, the rescue group should divide to provide assistance to both the people on the Lipkin and those descending from Razdelny Pass.

The Soviets agreed to our assessments and recommendations, by now too overwhelmed by the staggering sequence of events to dispute, and apparently trusting our objectivity in a situation that involved a good many of our own teammates.

At 8:30 P.M. on the sixth, Shataeyeva came on the air again and the roar of the storm at various moments simply obliterated her transmission; the wind seemed to snatch her voice away from time to time, but the message was all too clear. Two more of the women, the youngest two, had died in the last three hours. One more of their tents had been shattered by the wind, and five of them were in the tent without poles on a ledge they had scooped out of the steep ridge.

They were taking turns going outside of the collapsed tent and trying to dig into the hard wind-blown snow of the ridge. The snow under the surface was granular and very loose and did not submit to the forming of a cave. It was like digging in a tub of dry loose sand.

Elvira was clearly beside herself with grief, yet she somehow maintained an almost eerie composure, talking calmly about problems with the tents, no stoves, no water, faltering only when she referred to her dead companions. We remembered the lady interpreter's comment of just that morning—Elvira had seemed to have entered a dream.

It snowed another six inches at Base through the night of the sixth. By early morning of August 7, the temperature had dropped to around 22 degrees F. The Achik Tash appeared as it would look in winter. Elvira came on the radio at about 8:00 A.M. She sounded very weak, very tired, and distinctly disoriented. She repeated herself as she tried to describe the night just passed. They were all very cold, they had eaten nothing for a day and a half, and they had little strength left.

Abalakov pressed her, trying to determine whether they were still trying to descend to the Lipkin ridge. She hesitated, did not answer the question directly, but said almost fiercely, "Three more are sick; now there are only two of us who are functioning, and we are getting weaker. We cannot, we would not leave our comrades after all they have done for us. We are Soviet women. We must stick together, whatever happens!"

Abalakov knew well what was taking place and that whoever remained of his "girls" had little time left before their strength to go down would be totally exhausted. He again tried alternate haranguing and gentle persuasion to

202

get them to abandon their hopeless position on the ridge, but by that time the pattern of their agony seemed irreversible. In the spirit of group solidarity, they were committed to stand by each "sick" teammate; and, as they did so, one by one they began to die themselves.

As Abalakov kept the main transceiver open for instant communication with the women, we reached Jed Williamson and Peter Lev at Camp III with a Sony transmitter the Dutch team had brought. We apprised them of the overall situation involving the Soviet women and the lack of any communication from Jock Glidden's group. We stated that the weather forecast was for even worse weather for the next two days. We noted that Georg and Viktor had earlier reported that tents had been destroyed and that food and fuel supplies were crucially low. In the face of all this, we asked them how they felt about things. Through Jed, we gathered that Peter's position was that any party descending from Camp III under the current conditions was "in the most dire danger of becoming caught in an avalanche and, if not buried, getting lost in the blizzard during the descent."

Jed seemed to lean toward descending and reported that several others felt the same way; and thus it was left that when they decided what they were going to do and if they decided to go down, they should call Base. In the meantime, on the chance that they might decide to descend immediately, a support party would leave Camp II that day to help guide them down. John Evans and the support group from Base should arrive at Camp I that evening. They would join Bruce Carson at I. Early in the morning, John and Bruce and anyone else who was available would leave for Camp II to back up Valodya. All the other rescuers would proceed toward the Lipkin ridge. In the meantime, Valodya would leave Camp II immediately and begin placing wand markers in the snow from Camp II upward toward III. The Russians instructed Valodya to proceed with whomever he could persuade to go in the direction of Razdelny Pass. It was urged that he try to communicate by radio with Georg and Viktor every hour and, failing that, by voice signals.

Elvira came back on the air at 10:00 A.M. The roar of the wind was almost constant as she transmitted, but several standing nearest the receiver thought they could hear one of the women weeping.

"We are holding on. We cannot dig in; we are too weak. We have had almost nothing to eat or drink for two days. The three girls are going rapidly. It is very sad here where it was once so beautiful."

Her voice broke and she sobbed for the briefest moment, then regained her composure and said in a tremendously weary but steady voice, "We will carry on and talk again soon. Over."

We asked one another, How could they have survived so long? Thirty to 40 degrees below zero, consuming wind, no tents, no food. What keeps them going? Why do those smiling, happy, cheerful women have to die?

It snowed intermittently but hard through the morning at Base. The mess tent was crammed to overflowing with people from the many nationalities who made up the International Camp. We continued to wonder what could be happening to Steck, Glidden, and Wren. The real (perhaps the only) hope of the day lay in Evans and Valodya giving assistance to the large group retreating from Camp III.

Shataeyeva came on again at noon. One more had died. Four were dead. Two were dying. The condition of the last two we could only guess. The transmission was brief. Elvira almost seemed delirious, but she said, "We will go down; there is nothing left for us here. They are all gone now. The last asked, 'When will we see the flowers again?' The others earlier asked about the children. Now it is no use. We will go down."

The mountain was totally closed in by clouds, and the

great wind roared across the ridges high and low. At Base we could just see across the valley, nothing above. The wind was gusting to 40 miles an hour across the meadow, and the temperature remained around 28 degrees. In zero visibility, with the possibility of descending to the right and over the huge east face or to the left and onto the not so precipitous but avalanching north face, the dying Soviet women had run out of alternatives. It was only a matter of hours; and though no word was spoken, virtually every person in camp hoped they would be mercifully few.

There was no transmission at 2:00 P.M. from Elvira, and we wondered if they were moving down or if the end had come. The receiver had been on continuously since 6:00 A.M., so the batteries were changed to ensure that there was no failure either in transmission or receiving.

The rescue group called in from Camp I and reported that Jeff Lowe, the Englishmen, and the French were going to try to go up with Kostya and Boris to the ice cave camp on the Lipkin. We briefed them on the status of the women and reminded them we were still concerned for the Siberians, Japanese, and Americans.

Roskelley had contracted diarrhea and would remain at Camp I with Frank Sarnquist. Frank would treat the sick as they came down off the mountain.

Evans was on his way to Camp II with Bruce Carson, who had joined the rescue group at Camp I. One of the Swiss named Hans had joined up as well. They were to support Valodya and assist the large group descending from Camp III.

The Japanese on the Lipkin had been in touch with their people at Base, but not with anyone else. They must have been transmitting on a different frequency than any of the other groups, since their voices were not heard on the communication tent receiver. Nor did the Japanese at Base make known until somewhat later that their four men on the Lipkin had heard the transmission from the Russian women and, though they spoke no Russian, sensed something was wrong. When this was confirmed by the Japanese at Base, two of the four set out to try to rescue the women. The storm was so violent and visibility so limited, the wind chill factor so great and loss of location of their own camp so likely, that they were forced to turn back after getting only a short distance. Several times in the attempt they were blown off their feet. They were probably less than 1,500 yards from the women when they started.

The barriers of language and cultural differences in judgments of value and importance within those barriers added the final sense of confusion to the International Camp. The Russians may never have known about these transmissions, but they never revealed it if they did; nor did they suggest at any point a tie-in with the rescue effort being mounted from Base. Most likely in the great confusion of large numbers of people in apparent trouble, they didn't know. In the face of the frightful conditions, it is significant that the Japanese on the Lipkin even tried to reach the Soviet women.

Elvira came on the air at 3:30 P.M. She spoke incoherently and then seemed to have lost track of time and referred to the illness of two of the women who had already died. The sound of the storm had momentarily eased, and someone beside her (Valentina?) was audibly weeping. Then Elvira began to sob. "They are all dead; what will happen to us? What will happen to the children? [The two women who had youngsters had already died.] It is not fair, we did everything right."

Abalakov sat at the transmitter cutting in, trying to console Shataeyeva. "Viretska, my dear, beautiful girl, you have been very brave, all of you. Please hold on, we are trying to reach you."

Elvira came back on calmer, but distinctly weaker than she was three hours earlier. "We are sorry, we have failed you. We tried so hard. Now we are so cold."

"Elvira, don't give up. Stay awake; try to move your

limbs. Kostya and Boris and others are trying to reach you. Keep calling us on the radio. We will not leave the receiver." The sad, thin-faced lady interpreter did a brave job of keeping us informed of the conversation as, frequently on the edge of tears, she helped us understand that Abalakov was not cynically trying to raise the hopes of his doomed friends, but simply trying to make their deaths seem less forlorn. He felt that anything he could do to ease the anguish of their slow and certain dying was a merciful thing.

The transmission at 5:00 P.M. was garbled, but we sensed one more had died, leaving three still alive. The storm seemed to be continuing to build in intensity, and for a brief moment we caught a glimpse of the clouds racing across Krylenko Pass. We estimated the wind velocity at 80 to 100 miles per hour.

Farther below, Kostya and Oleg called in to report they could make no progress in the storm. They were worried about the large group of Siberians which was descending, but thought they were safely below the upper ridge line and thus somewhat protected from the most punishing winds. They said they would go up in the morning with the rescue team, whom they could now see below in breaks in the storm.

At 6:00 P.M., we got the tremendously cheering report that the entire group from Camp III had made it down to Camp II and that some were continuing down to Camp I. It was thought that Heidi Ludi, Anya, and Sepp Schwankener had fairly serious frostbite and would need medical assistance if not helicopter evacuation from Camp I. Everyone else was apparently okay.

At 6:30, we heard several clicks of the transmitter key and then above the roar of the wind the very faint voice of Elvira. "Another has died. We cannot go through another night. I do not have the strength to hold down the transmitter button."

At this, the Russian lady interpreter burst into tears. People looked at one another in embarrassed silence. We saw Zina, the Russian camp dietitian who had been so kind to all the Americans, across the meadow with tears streaming down her face.

At 8:30, the receiver registered a few of the clicks we heard earlier and then Elvira came on in a voice almost drained of passion. "Now we are two. And now we will all die. We are very sorry. We tried but we could not . . . Please forgive us. We love you. Goodbye."

The radio clicked off, and everyone in that storm-lashed meadow knew the cheerful Soviet "girls" were gone forever. Everyone in the meadow wept unashamedly as the fact of finality was driven home by the utter silence of the radio and the unforgiving wind. The Soviet men and women wept the hardest and caused the rest of us to weep even more as they, several Russian generations removed from the Church, made the sign of the cross and with that almost forbidden gesture signified the end had come. And then there was only the wind.

CHAPTER ELEVEN
▲
The Edelweiss and the Cross

As the crowd at Base gathered around the radio hearing the last transmission of Elvira, the rescue team of Doug Scott; Tut Braithwaite; Jeff Lowe; the two Soviet coaches, Boris and Kostya; and the four French climbers, Bernard, Yves, Benoit and Michel, had arrived at Camp I below the Lipkin ridge. Jeff recollects those moments spent 5,000 feet below the women:

> For the benefit of Doug, Tut, and me, Boris translates the message that is crackling through the radio: From the camp of the Russian women on the summit we hear the news that "The others are all dead—I am too weak to push the button on the radio any longer—this is my last transmission—good-bye."
>
> So, our efforts have been in vain—we knew they were useless when we left base camp. But this is too much. The last woman is dying tonight, several thousand feet above us. She's dying and we are powerless to help her. Boris tells us that his (and our) comrade in the cave, Kostya, was engaged to be married to one of those poor women. When I look into

Kostya's eyes across the candle-lit cave, our lack of a common language is no barrier to communication; the anguish is evident.

What is there to say? Kostya has lost his fiancée. We have all lost a hopeless struggle to be of help. Eight women lost their lives.

Almost as if he had prepared for this moment Tut produces a bottle of Scotch from nowhere. A toast to the Russian ladies. The toast has words, but they are forgettable. What won't be forgotten by those who were there that night on Peak Lenin was the ambience that developed under those desperate and melancholy conditions. We drank a little. We smoked away the harsh realities with which we were dealing.

We talked. Not mainly about death, but about other things, like: What is it like to live in Russia? America? Europe? Are you a member of the Communist Party? Do you like the job you have? Do you have a family? What are they like? The questions were like those that any new acquaintances might ask, but the answers were unusually open, honest, and frank.

We got to know each other that night in some very important ways. We walked together on paths that are normally closed to strangers. We all felt the common bond of the human condition. I was glad to have these particular people to share this dark situation with. I saw the light in the souls of a few strong individuals shining through a rent in the clouds of a thunderstorm.

The death of the Soviet women numbed everyone's awareness of the storm, which continued to build until it reached its peak about 10:00 P.M. It was difficult to focus on the plight of Chris, Al, and Jock, whom we knew were camped somewhere up there above 21,000 feet. I damned and double-damned Soviet customs for having confiscated our radios. It was not inconceivable, in light of the fate of the Soviet women, that they too had perished in the storm. The recurring and reassuring thought was of the collective experience of the three climbers.

I went by Monastyrski's tent, and we looked at each other for some time. He pulled out a bottle of brandy, and we drank from mess cups in silence. He finally said, "We did everything possible, Robert—now this."

I returned at midnight to my tent, thinking we must inform Evans and the others on the first radio call in the morning that all the Soviet women had died and that we did not know anything about Jock's group. We wanted them to remain on the mountain until we knew something more. It was now quite cold in Base—perhaps 15 degrees below zero Fahrenheit. At the top of Lenin? It could easily have been 40 to 50 below.

I awakened around 2:00 A.M. The Soviet Army two-man mountain tent was stiff with ice. It was bitterly cold. I forced the frozen toggled flaps apart and I remembered the "girls," their tents, and their deaths. Up the valley it was sparklingly clear, the sky daylight bright with stars, the landscape totally plastered with the new snow, looking like winter, while the winds aloft continued to roar. The upper levels of the peaks were cloaked in blowing snow.

It was hard to think in positive terms of our friends' night on Lenin, for the storm had been so staggering in its force that our convictions about their well-being were extremely shaky. I was afraid of what daylight might reveal, and I took a Seconal to numb any further thought about anything.

The tent was showering down droplets of water on my sleeping bag as I woke at 8:15 A.M. A blinding sun now beat down. In the soggy mess of the Base Camp quadrangle it was quickly apparent that though the sun was melting the snow on every surface it touched, it was still very cold. As I looked up at Lenin, the whole mountain was clear, and the northeast ridge was characterized by snow plumes blowing high into the sky. Great billowing gusts of snow raced across the ridge from the northwest. I clocked the blowing clouds over a series of estimated distance segments, and they checked out at 70, 80, and 85 miles per hour. It continued to be dangerous up there.

We reached John Evans at Camp I. He had gone to Camp II from Base and back down to I the night before. Everyone was safe from Camp III and many would reach Base before the day was over. Heidi Ludi had fairly serious frostbite of the hands and some in her feet, but her spirit was good considering what she had been through. Anya was okay but with a small amount of frostbite, and Sepp Schwankener, who had been a great help to Peter Lev in the rescue effort, had some frostbite in his hands. Frank Sarnquist recommended sending a helicopter up to Camp I for the more seriously afflicted. He said they would stamp out a landing pad.

Evans reported that the Siberians were now coming down off the Lipkin and that they had seen the Americans in the afternoon of August 5. They seemed fine. Somehow there was a bit of hope in that, but the last three days of giant storm had to change the odds somewhat. The Siberians also seemed to be indicating something that did not square with Ronnie Richards's account of August 5; namely, that they felt the women were leaving for the summit on the sixth. They claimed to have seen them on the fifth. Perhaps in all the storm and confusion on the mountain the Siberians got their dates confused. Perhaps, too, the women left for the summit from their high camp later than anyone imagined.

By midmorning the wind along the summit ridge of Lenin had begun to let up. We borrowed the powerful 850 x 15 glasses the Englishmen had brought along and began to grid the upper Lipkin and summit ridges in search of Jock and the Japanese. There was a strong possibility we wouldn't find anything. Working down the summit ridge there were a couple of dark spots in the snow that could have been rocks, or—the thought that they might have been bodies had an eerie unreality about it. Farther down the ridge, no sign. No tents visible on the Lipkin. Much farther down and on a different ridge, five climbers were descending; but they were too low and too far from the line of ascent to be our friends. They had to be the last of the Siberians.

At about 10:30 A.M., emerging from the shadow of the north face and diagonally left up a snow slope leading to the summit ridge, three figures moving together appeared. "There they are! They're okay!" There was a scramble for the glasses, first John Marts, then Molly, and finally Pete, who passed the glasses back, beaming with relief. In a few more minutes, four more climbers were to appear to the right of the three—also heading up for the summit ridge. They had to be the Japanese.

Shortly after we had spotted the two teams climbing toward the summit of Lenin, Abalakov came to our sector of the camp, smiled faintly as we told him the good news, and took the glasses for a personal look.

"Perhaps they will find the 'girls,' but it really doesn't matter—after all, they are finished, aren't they!" The rocklike old man wandered across the meadow to the memorial we had been building (with his considerable assistance) for Gary Ullin. In a very short time the unique solitary rock with its large cruciform cross of heavy stones originally erected in Gary's memory had become a tribute to fifteen dead climbers, nine of them women.

The two ropes proceeded in unison toward the summit pyramid, and we wondered how much longer it would be before they stopped. It was not long. As we observed the seven climbers milling around in the saddle below the final summit ridge, there was great commotion at the communication tent. We arrived as Al's voice came through saying, "Bahza, this is Sasha Four. This is Allen Steck. We are transmitting on the Japanese radio. Something very strange, something very sad has happened here." They had arrived. Al's voice came slowly; they were above

23,000 feet and literally in the midst of a summit attempt and they had stumbled on a tragedy of which they had no forewarning. The Japanese did not speak enough English to give them any notion of what had befallen the Soviet women. "We have found one of the Russian women frozen. I suppose the rest are above, there are signs farther up the slope. We will communicate in a few minutes as we get higher up. Please stand by. Over."

We acknowledged Al's transmission with great relief and asked them to determine what they could about the death of the women, but above all to get down off the mountain safely. They had come upon Elvira's body stretched out as if sleeping, face up, in the small saddle below the summit on the north side. She appeared to be asleep. Her face was composed and peaceful. Chris Wren commented later that he recognized the striking face of Elvira and realized an unbelievable tragedy had occurred.

Steck was back on the transmitter in about a half hour; it was 12:30 P.M., and he said in a now distinctly shocked voice, "We found two more, half buried in drifting snow and above them what appears to be three more ladies. Above us is another, apparently in a belay position with a rope leading down the slope. It is pretty grim. We will go on up to the top and see if we can locate the eighth."

Al asked us to put Eugene Gippenreiter on the radio. "Eugene, we are stunned by the magnitude of this tragedy. . . . We share in your grief over the loss of the girls. Over and out." Al recalls that as they probed among the wreckage and the bodies, he wept and then climbed higher.

Glidden noted in his diary: "As we climbed higher we came across more stations of horror—one group of three huddled together—tent obviously swept away. Then the seventh and highest leaning over sleeping on tent material as if belaying the others below—we stepped over their belay rope."

They went on to the summit, where they found no trace of the eighth woman. It was not until Elvira's husband, Vladimir, went up with a support team seven days later that the eighth was found buried in the ruins of a tent under the four bodies previously discovered.

The two teams descended off Peak Lenin past the bodies of the women at about 2:30 P.M. to conclude one of the strangest and most tragic episodes in mountaineering history. They had too little energy in reserve to do anything about the bodies save place dowel wand markers around them. We at Base had strongly admonished them to get off the mountain as quickly and safely as possible.

Even as the dramatic events had been unfolding high on Lenin, members of the American team not involved in the rescue attempt were putting in many hours chiseling an inscription in the great rock commemorating Gary's loss, but which had become, as well, a memorial to all the fallen climbers of the summer of 1974.

The inscription said simply, "In memory of Jon Gary Ullin, who died in avalanche, on 19th Party Congress Peak, July 25, 1974. A graceful man." The cross, erected on top of the great rock by Abalakov and made with 75- to 100-pound flat rocks hauled up on the rock by several of us, had transformed the remote and beautiful meadow from a scenic sheep pasture into an international memorial.

Helicopters began arriving on Thursday afternoon, August 8. One was a sleek turboprop carrying the assistant to the Minister of Sports. It never seems to take very long for inquests to get under way. Word quickly spread that an investigation was about to begin into the deaths of Gary Ullin, Eva Eissenschmidt, the Estonians, and (most important to the stunned Russians and Kirghiz) the Soviet women. Others would arrive the next day for the inquiry and there was rampant speculation among the international teams as to what the proceedings would yield.

215

Some thought Abalakov would be blamed for letting the women attempt the traverse of Lenin, especially in light of the opposition among the conservatives of the Soviet Federation of Mountaineering. One sensed the Soviets might be caught on the horns of their own dilemma—either they were for equality of women in the eyes of the international climbing delegations or they were not. Others thought it was a pro forma procedure, necessary to establish a sense of Soviet solidarity in the face of the tragic series of events that had befallen the Pamirs camp.

The tribunal went on for a number of hours. As it turned out, Abalakov was vindicated because he had ordered the women to turn back at least a day before their ordeal began. The official gathering concluded that the Soviet women had been unavoidably overwhelmed by an unprecedented storm and that all the others died in circumstances over which they had no control.

The Soviet women died because of a combination of faulty judgment, inadequate equipment, and obvious bad luck. If they had not been warned of an impending storm of major proportions and had not been admonished to retreat or remain in a secure position, their decision to continue their traverse of Lenin (which in turn determined their decision to camp on the summit) would have been at least understandable.

They never revealed their reasons for moving up to the summit in the face of the storm. They could have been running low on rations and decided to make a run for it rather than risk laying siege by waiting out a large storm with insufficient supplies. They may have reasoned that they would never get a second chance once the storm of the predicted magnitude struck.

Their decision to camp on the summit of Lenin, taken with the failure of the tents and the unprecedented storm, removed virtually any chance of escape. The tents the Soviet women were using simply failed. We knew from our experience with tents of the same design at Base that they were not adequate for more than moderate winds, that the tent poles collapsed under modest snow loads, and that the closure system would not prevent blowing snow from seeping in and filling the interiors.

Once the tents failed the first night and some of the women began to die of hypothermia, they lost whatever chance they might have had to effect a successful retreat, for they would not leave any of their teammates behind so long as they were alive. Thus, struggling to survive in the storm, but losing strength hour by hour, they died one by one in the unrelenting wind and snow.

Psychological and physiological deterioration at high altitude is still imperfectly understood. It seems judgment is one of the most acutely affected cognitive processes, especially when combined with the stress to survive. Climbers have done strange things in such situations: gloves have been forgotten at the price of frostbite; oxygen valves have been left closed during periods of crucial need; climbing and logistical strategies have been ignored. Some of these forces may also have worked against the Soviet women in subtle ways.

Equally, the psychological force of their commitment to demonstrate that Soviet women were a strong and perhaps special breed (which no one ever doubted) had its ultimate effect on the situation. It robbed them of the flexibility that is so vital in making prudent decisions on high mountains. In a sense, once they had announced to the Scots on the summit, "We are strong. We are Soviet women. We will camp here and go down in the morning," they never really had a chance.

The Soviet women died climbing alpine-style on an extremely cold, very high peak under what had become siege conditions, insufficiently understood by them. They had all of the above factors working against them plus a storm of the greatest ferocity in the memory of the oldest Kirghiz.

When Elvira said, "We are sorry we have failed you," she and the others had really only failed in the understanding that humans are at best only privileged trespassers on high mountains. There is no real conquest beyond a kind of convergence of self and the mountain, and a realization that even on the most brilliantly planned and executed ascents luck is always a major factor.

▲

The evening of August 8, Jock, Al, and Chris settled in their sleeping bags and pondered the confusing day. The wind had diminished to a modest level. They had eaten little; they had no appetite despite the long day on the summit. It had not been a jubilant arrival on top, and now they were back in camp still unclear about the grim events that had taken place above. All night long, between fits of restless sleep, they were convinced they heard women's voices outside the tent.

Jock Glidden's diary tersely reconstructs the end of the strange episode: "We return to our collapsed tent—repitch it, have supper and all swear we hear strident feminine voices outside (ghosts of the women)—but it's only the wind in the tent's rigging."

Everybody came down from Peak Lenin in the renewed sunlight of August 9. We prepared for a mass memorial service to be held at the great rock. Jock, Al, and Chris came in looking worn but fit. It was a great relief to see them safely back.

As these last climbers returned, there was a feeling of ending, of conclusion. The summer that had begun so well —and that had been an unbroken disaster from the avalanche on Krylenko to Gary's death, the deaths of the Estonians and Eva Eissenschmidt, and now the staggering loss of the eight Soviet women—would end in funeral. The entire camp was in a state of inexpressible shock.

Early in the morning on August 10, at about 7:00 A.M.,

we were literally tossed about on the ground in our second major earthquake. The ground rolled and undulated, and huge avalanches tumbled off all the major faces of the high peaks. The quake was unnerving. There seemed to be no end to unfriendly natural phenomena in the Pamirs.

At noon, all the people in Base Camp gathered at the great rock for a memorial service to honor the climbers who had died. A Russian woman said of the eight who had died on Peak Lenin, "They were happy gifted women climbers with many heartbroken families and friends left behind. They were simply overwhelmed by natural forces beyond their control."

A Swiss noted that Eva Eissenschmidt never expected to climb so high and died amid the beauty she captured with her talented camera.

We observed that Gary Ullin had been very happy in the Pamirs and that he died doing what he liked to do best.

We said the Americans could not adequately express their feelings of sorrow over the loss of the Soviet women, the Estonians, and Eva Eissenschmidt. As the memorial came to a close, Peak Nineteen and Mount Lenin sparkled in the brilliant sunshine beyond the great rock. The sun backlighted the cruciform cross erected by Abalakov and the Americans, and despite the almost arctic cold of the recent days, the edelweiss of the meadow seemed once again to have come back to life.

▲

The heavy quakes continued to jar us for the next three days. We wished that our departure time could be advanced. It was just as well that it wasn't, as Gary's parents arrived on August 12 in an Aeroflot helicopter, accompanied by a Kirghiz interpreter and an official of the Federation of Mountaineering. The trip had been arranged by United Airlines in cooperation with Pan American and Aeroflot. Chet and Phyllis Ullin had come the 12,000 miles to pay their final respects to their son. Our awareness of Gary's loss deepened with the presence of his grieving parents.

A final memorial was held at the great rock attended only by the Americans and four Englishmen to whom we had grown close. We formed a circle and held hands as Phyllis Ullin requested. The Twenty-third Psalm was read from the Bible we had borrowed from our friends from Grenoble, and Chet Ullin, tears streaming down his face, sang one of Gary's favorite boyhood songs, "I Want to Wake Up in the Mountains." The Ullins pulled apart from the circle, went to the rock, and, still holding hands, wept before the inscription to Gary. There was little emotion left in any of us. We simply wanted to leave the Pamirs and return home.

▲

When the final earthquake hit, the grassy meadow undulated and shook and we were again tossed about in our sleeping bags. The faraway roar of falling ice filled the air and dozens of heads poked out of tents to look up in the valley. The whole of the Krylenko face and the north face of Peak Nineteen and its northeast and northwest buttresses were crashing down in a last stupendous series of avalanches. The dust of the pulverized ice and snow hung in the air for minutes, and the sheep on the mountainside above Base had hunched together in a tight band and appeared with one mournful voice to express the nameless hostility of that moment and that strange and beautiful place.

▲
Glossary

ADIABATICALLY. Referring to adiabatic cooling and heating of the air as an air mass is lifted over a mountain range. The drop in temperature with altitude, or dry adiabatic lapse rate, is about 5 degrees for each 1,000 feet.

ARREST. To bring oneself to a stop from a sliding or tumbling position on a snow slope by applying pressure to the pick or the adze of one's ice axe.

BELAY. To provide security for a moving climber by means of a rope and a stable position for the belayer.

BERGSCHRUND (SCHRUND). The uppermost crevasse which is created when the flowing ice of a glacier moves away from the stationary rock, snow, or ice above.

CAGOULE. A roomy knee-length pullover parka, often used over down undergarments for bivouacking.

CARABINER. An oval metal link, about three inches long, that opens like a safety pin and is generally used to attach the climbing rope or the climber to belay anchors or intermediate points of protection.

CLEAN CLIMBING. Climbing in which protection is achieved not by driving pitons into cracks but by placing steel or aluminum non-deforming chocks or "nuts" in rock deformations.

221

COULOIRS. Generally, gullies or waste chutes in mountain faces down which snow, rock, and ice are discharged during thawing or heavy rain or snowfall.

COL. A pass or saddle leading from one side of a mountain or ridge system to another.

CRAMPONS. A set of steel spikes that are strapped to the soles of the climbing boots to prevent slipping on hard snow or ice. Crampons generally are made with ten or twelve spikes (points) per boot (see *Frontpoint*).

EXPANSION BOLT. A bolt which physically expands when driven into a hole drilled in the rock. Expansion bolts provide anchors on otherwise flawless, anchorless sections of rock.

FRONTPOINT. A technique used to climb steep ice or hard snow. The climber uses the horizontally angled front points of the twelve-point crampon, kicking the points into the snow or ice and standing on them.

FRONTPOINT IN TRAVERSE. To use the frontpoint technique to move sideways instead of up.

GLISSADING. Sliding on one's feet on firm snow in the manner of skiing, using the ice axe shaft as a brake where necessary.

HYPOTHERMIA. A lowering of the body's core temperature caused by a combination of low air temperature, moisture, wind, and fatigue, with the resultant impairment of body functions, loss of coordination, and eventually consciousness.

ICE AXE ARREST. A technique used to stop a slide or fall on snow. The climber jams the pick of the ice axe into the snow while holding the shaft of the axe diagonally across his or her chest.

ICE SCREWS. Sturdy solid or tubular screws, at least six inches long, designed to be hammered and screwed into ice to act as an anchor or point of protection.

JUMAR. A mechanical device used to ascend an anchored rope by means of a ratchet system which jams against the rope when weight is applied and slides upward when free of weight. *To jumar* is to use a mechanical device to ascend a rope.

LEAD. To be first on the rope while climbing—thus to climb without an overhead belay. The person belaying the leader is sometimes called the *second*.

LEADS. The division of a climb into sections defined by how far the leader climbs before anchoring and belaying the second.

222

The length of a lead is determined by the rope length or the availability of good anchors. Also called *pitches*.

NEVE FIELD. An area on a glacier that is covered by perennial granular snow which eventually compacts into glacial ice. Also called *firn*.

PINS. A slang term for pitons, which are metal spikes of varying size and shape. They are driven into cracks in the rock and used for anchor points.

RAPPEL. A method of descending by sliding down an anchored rope. Friction is employed either by wrapping the rope around the climber's body or passing it through a mechanical system attached to the climber to help slow and control the descent.

SCHRUND. See *Bergschrund*.

SCREE. Small loose fairly uniform pebbles sometimes several feet in depth, the rubble formed of rock decay on newer and volcanic mountains.

SERAC. A large block or pinnacle of ice on a glacier—formed by the melting or movement of the glacier.

STIRRUP SLINGS. Sometimes called *etriers*, a ladderlike device made of webbing and used in aid climbing to stand in or ascend.

TIE OFF A LOOP. To tie a loop in the climbing rope in order to attach the climber to an anchor with a carabiner.

WAIST SLING. Webbing wrapped and tied around the waist. This becomes the point of attachment of the rope to the climber— usually more comfortable than merely tying the rope around the waist.

WARTHOG. A type of ice screw.

WATER ICE. Ice formed from freezing layers of water or melted snow. A very hard, brittle type of ice.

WHITEOUT. Conditions of fog, clouds, or blowing snow that render visibility and orientation almost impossible.